W9-BKM-303

Experiments in effective writing

domains
in language and composition

Experiments in effective writing

VICTOR E. GOULD

HARCOURT BRACE JOVANOVICH, INC.

New York Chicago San Francisco Atlanta Dallas

Victor E. Gould did his undergraduate work in English at Whitworth College in Spokane. In 1965, under the auspices of the National Defense Education Act, he attended the English Institute at the University of Washington in Seattle, where he first became interested in the work of Francis Christensen. For the past eleven years he has taught English in the State of Washington, and is currently teaching at the Auburn High School in Auburn.

Copyright © 1972 by Harcourt Brace Jovanovich, Inc.

All rights reserved. No part of this publication
may be reproduced or transmitted in any form
or by any means, electronic or mechanical, including
photocopy, recording or any information storage and retrieval system,
without permission in writing from the publisher.

Printed in the United States of America.

ISBN   0–15–312318–4

ACKNOWLEDGMENTS: For permission to reprint copyrighted material, grateful acknowledgment is made to the following sources:

HOLLIS ALPERT and SATURDAY REVIEW: Review of "Fantastic Journey" by Hollis Alpert from *Saturday Review*, April 20, 1968, copyright 1968 Saturday Review, Inc.

APPLETON-CENTURY-CROFTS, DIVISION OF MEREDITH PUBLISHING COMPANY: From *The Red Badge of Courage* by Stephen Crane, 1895, published by D. Appleton Co. From *A Program For Effective Writing* by Robert L. Shurter and James M. Reid, published by Appleton-Century-Crofts, 1966.

ATLANTIC-LITTLE BROWN AND COMPANY: From *Mutiny on the Bounty* by Charles Nordhoff and James Norman Hall.

THE BOBBS-MERRILL COMPANY, INC.: From *Lie Down in Darkness* by William Styron, coyright © 1951, by William Styron. From *Understanding and Using English* by Newman P. Birk and Genevieve B. Birk, copyright © 1949, 1951, 1958, 1965, by The Odyssey Press, Inc.

BRANDT & BRANDT: From *Nineteen Eighty Four* by George Orwell, copyright, 1949 by Harcourt Brace Jovanovich, Inc.

HAROLD BRODKEY C/O INTERNATIONAL FAMOUS AGENCY: "First Love and Other Sorrows" by Harold Brodkey from *The New Yorker*, June 15, 1957, copyright © 1957 by Harold Brodkey.

COLLEGE ENTRANCE EXAMINATION BOARD, NEW YORK: From *Freedom and Discipline in English: Report of the Commission*, published in 1965 by the College Entrance Examination Board, New York. From the *Moniteur* of France, March, 1815 from *End-of-Year Examinations in English for College-Bound Students Grades 9-12. A Project-Report by the Commission on English*, published in 1963 by the College Entrance Examination Board, New York.

COLLINS-KNOWLTON WING, INC.: From "R.M.S. *Titanic*" by Hanson W. Baldwin from *Harper's* Magazine, January 1934, copyright © 1933 by Harper & Row, Publishers, Inc.; renewed © 1961.

CORNELL UNIVERSITY PRESS: From "Out for Stars: A Meditation on Robert Frost" from *Poetry and Civilization* by George Frisbie Whicher, copyright 1955 by Cornell University Press.

CURTIS BROWN, LTD.: From "Everybody's Sport" by John Knowles from *Holiday* Magazine, July 1956, copyright © 1956 by the Curtis Publishing Co., Inc.

DODD, MEAD & COMPANY, INC.: From "Winged Bullets" from *Grassroot Jungles* by Edwin Way Teale. From "The Finish of Patsy Barnes" by Paul Laurence Dunbar.

DOUBLEDAY & COMPANY, INC.: From *Up From Slavery* by Booker T. Washington. From *The Agony and the Ecstasy* by Irving Stone, copyright © 1961 by Doubleday & Company, Inc.

DOUBLEDAY & COMPANY, INC. and VALLENTINE, MITCHELL & CO. LTD. as the Canadian publishers: From *The Diary of a Young Girl* by Anne Frank, copyright 1952 by Otto H. Frank. Published in Canada under the title *The Diary of Anne Frank*.

CONSTANCE GARLAND DOYLE and ISABEL GARLAND LORD: From "Under the Lion's Paw" by Hamlin Garland.

NORMA MILLAY ELLIS: From "Ashes of Life" by Edna St. Vincent Millay from *Collected Poems*, Harper & Row, copyright 1917, 1945 by Edna St. Vincent Millay.

ESQUIRE, INC.: From "Snowfall in Childhood" by Ben Hecht.

JANE RYDER FISHER: From "The City of Refuge" by Rudolph Fisher from *American Negro Short Stories* by John Henrik Clarke.

FOLLETT PUBLISHING COMPANY: From *The Lively Art of Writing* by Lucille Vaughan Payne, copyright © 1965 by Follett Publishing Company.

HARPER & ROW, PUBLISHERS, INC., MRS. LAURA HUXLEY and CHATTO AND WINDUS LTD.: from pp. 58-59 (hardbound edition) in *Brave New World Revisited* by Aldous Huxley (Harper & Row, 1958).

SYDNEY HARRIS: From "All's Trite with the World" by Sydney J. Harris from the *Chicago Daily News*, January 16, 1946 reprinted in *Building Better English, 12* by John J. De Boer, published by Harper & Row Publishers, Inc.

HOUGHTON MIFFLIN COMPANY: From *Shane* by Jack Schaefer.

ALEXANDER R. JAMES, LITERARY EXECUTOR OF WILLIAM JAMES: From "The Moral Equivalent of War" by William James.

ALFRED A. KNOPF, INC.: From "Wounds" from *Heroic Love* by Edward Loomis, copyright © 1960 by Edward Loomis. From *The Wall* by John Hersey, copyright, 1950, by John Hersey. From *The Cruel Sea* by Nicholas Monsarrat, copyright 1951 by Nicholas Monsarrat. From *The Sea of Grass* by Conrad Richter, copyright 1936 by The Curtis Publishing Company. From "Paul's Case" from *Youth and the Bright Medusa* by Willa Cather, copyright, 1920, by Willa Cather.

J. B. LIPPINCOTT COMPANY: From *To Kill a Mockingbird* by Harper Lee, copyright, ©, 1960 by Harper Lee.

LITTLE BROWN AND COMPANY: From *Bare Feet in the Palace* by Agnes Newton Keith. From *All Quiet on the Western Front* by Erich Remarque.

THE MACMILLAN COMPANY and A. D. PETERS AND COMPANY: From *Darkness at Noon* by Arthur Koestler, copyright, 1941, by The Macmillan Company.

HAROLD MATSON COMPANY, INC.: "The Dragon" by Ray Bradbury, copyright 1958 by Ray Bradbury.

THE NEW YORK TIMES COMPANY: From "Review of Ayn Rand" by Nora Ephron from *The New York Times*, May 5, 1968, © 1968 by The New York Times Company. From "Behind the Credibility Gap" by David Schoenbrun from *The New York Times*, July 7, 1968, © 1968 by The New York Times Company.

OXFORD UNIVERSITY PRESS INC.: From "Who is Loyal to America?" from *Freedom, Loyalty, Dissent* by Henry Steele Commager, copyright 1954 by Oxford University Press, Inc.

PANTHEON BOOKS, A DIVISION OF RANDOM HOUSE, INC.: From *The Tin Drum* by Gunter Grass, © 1959 by Hermann Luchterhand Verlag GmbH, English translation © 1961, 1962 by Pantheon Books.

PUBLISHERS-HALL SYNDICATE: From "Dirt, Grime, and Cruel Crowding" by Eric Sevareid.

G. P. PUTNAM'S SONS: From *Bishop Walsh of Maryknoll* by Raymond Kerrison, © 1962 by Raymond Kerrison.

RANDOM HOUSE, INC.: From "Pure and Impure Poetry" from *Selected Essays of*

Robert Penn Warren, copyright 1943 by Robert Penn Warren. From "Nobel Prize Acceptance Speech" by William Faulkner from *The Faulkner Reader,* copyright 1954 by William Faulkner. From *The Dirty Dozen* by E. M. Nathanson, copyright © 1965 by E. M. Nathanson. From *Crime and Punishment* by Fyodor Dostoyevsky, copyright, 1950, by Random House, Inc. From "The Poet" by Isak Dinesen from *Seven Gothic Tales* by Isak Dinesen, copyright, 1934, by Harrison Smith and Robert Haas, Inc. From *Invisible Man* by Ralph Ellison, copyright 1947, 1948, 1952 by Ralph Ellison.

SATURDAY REVIEW: From "The Tradition of the Future" by Allan Nevins from *Saturday Review,* June 8, 1968, copyright 1968 Saturday Review, Inc.

SCHOCKEN BOOKS INC.: From "The Judgment" from *The Penal Colony* by Franz Kafka, copyright © 1948 by Schocken Books Inc.

CHARLES SCRIBNER'S SONS: From *Cry, The Beloved Country,* page 4, by Alan Paton, copyright 1948 Alan Paton. From *Ethan Frome,* page 8, by Edith Wharton, copyright 1911 Charles Scribner's Sons; renewal copyright 1939 Wm. R. Tyler. From "Big Two-Hearted River," copyright 1925 Charles Scribner's Sons; renewal copyright 1953 Ernest Hemingway, from *In Our Time,* pages 227, by Ernest Hemingway.

SEATTLE POST-INTELLIGENCER: From "Woman Acquitted as Strangler Missing" from *Seattle Post-Intelligencer,* July 21, 1968.

IRVING SHEPARD: From *The Sea Wolf* by Jack London.

SIMON & SCHUSTER.: From *The American Way of Death* by Jessica Mitford, copyright © 1963 by Jessica Mitford. From *The Decline of Pleasure* by Walter Kerr, © 1962 by Walter Kerr. From *Blackboard Jungle* by Evan Hunter, © 1954 by Evan Hunter.

THE VIKING PRESS INC.: From *Wolf Willow* by Wallace Stegner. From *Herzog* by Saul Bellow. From "A Company of Laughing Faces" from *Not For Publication and Other Stories* by Nadine Gordimer. From *The Grapes of Wrath* by John Steinbeck.

THE VIKING PRESS INC., ELIZABETH TAYLOR and CHATTO AND WINDUS LTD.: From "The First Death of Her Life" from *Hester Lilly and 12 Short Stories* by Elizabeth Taylor. Published in England titled *Hester Lilly and Other Stories.*

WADSWORTH PUBLISHING COMPANY, INC.: From *Words and Ideas* by Hans P. Guth, copyright 1965.

THE WELLS NEWS SERVICE, PRINCETON, N.J.: From "Some Questions of Values" by Charles A. Wells from *Between the Lines,* The Wells News Service, Princeton, N.J.

THE WORLD PUBLISHING COMPANY BY ARRANGEMENT WITH THE ESTATE OF THEODORE DREISER: From *Sister Carrie* by Theodore Dreiser.

Contents

Preface

The material in this text has been carefully selected and arranged in a way that relates directly to matters of style and rhetoric in the art of writing. At the heart of this material lies the concept of "productive rhetoric," a concept found in the "generative rhetoric" of Professor Francis Christensen, who, until his recent death, taught at the University of Southern California. Productive rhetoric explores the process of writing in a meaningful way, and, lacking the pseudo-intellectual atmosphere of some systems, stresses the naturalness of good writing through its emphasis on the principle of addition.

Assuming a competence in matters of correctness as handbook sections of grammars usually use the term, this course in composition places greatest emphasis on matters of effectiveness as they relate to style and writing maturity. Through an examination of the use of such elements as syntactic structures, semantic structures, and the concepts of productive rhetoric, the student sees a number of the possibilities that he can employ to advantage in the effective presentation of ideas and information, or, as it shall be called in this book, mature style.

But, before we can write prose with any maturity of style, we must spend some time considering those things that are capable of producing a mature style. And before we can competently analyze prose, we must take time to review basic syntactic elements so that we fully understand the relationships between the different parts of a sentence and the choices we have in the arranging of each of these elements. The appositive, the verb, the verbal, the parallelism, the absolute, the clause—these are the elements that usually give their names to sections of grammar books. But in those situations they are too often explained in isolation and exhibited as dry and sterile examples. Rather than isolate these syntactic structures, we need to see them as they are, the building blocks of mature writing, the creative devices that allow us to express facts and ideas with maximum effectiveness. Once we define these elements, we can illustrate them with carefully analyzed examples from the works of professional writers. The examples show that writers do, indeed, use these devices and, at the same time, they spell out the many ways in which writers can employ these devices to advantage. Then the student is asked to write on a certain topic, in order that he have a chance to experiment and to discover something of the variety and potential of each of these creative devices. This important factor, the selection of topics, has too often been subordinated or watered down by multiple choices. This book does not intend, however, to give a large number of possible writing topics. Rather, it will give just one in each case, one that has been proven successful, one that has produced an excellent response from students. Nevertheless, those who wish to experiment with topics that stimulate the imaginations and talents of particular students or class groups should do so.

Having considered the factors of mature style and having reviewed basic syntactic structures, we can immediately move on to a more meaningful examination of productive rhetoric. Three exercises in analysis supplement the study of each explanation and the examples pertaining to it. These should amply illustrate the basic principles of productive rhetoric. They, of course, in no way represent all the possibilities or all the innumerable examples with which our literature abounds. However, all examples are taken from the works of professional writers, in order to illustrate the validity of the principles of productive rhetoric.

One should have little difficulty in moving from the productive rhetoric of the sentence to that of the paragraph. Both the productive rhetoric of the sentence and the productive rhetoric of the paragraph show us clearly how and why writers group certain words and certain sentences in the way they do. In both the chapter on the sentence and the chapter on the paragraph, students will have a chance to write and to analyze their own material. This carries the theoretical into the realm of the practical, where the student can discover how and to what advantage he can group certain words or sentences.

A chapter on semantics follows those on sentence and paragraph rhetoric, giving the student an interesting look at his language, the manipulation of words, the overuse of certain words, and the creation of a living and constantly regenerating language.

The final chapter deals with evaluating the writing style of one well-known writer. If the elements described in this book are indeed the basic building materials of a mature style, then it should follow that writers skilled in the use of language can and do use them. If they do not, then the arguments put forward by this book collapse. To give the student a chance to evaluate this for himself, a project has been designed for a large-scale investigation of a single book. This project incorporates those elements, or criteria, discussed and worked with throughout this course. Again, others may wish to include additional elements in their investigations.

The appendices provide additional material to supplement two of the writing experiences in Chapter Five.

By showing the tremendous variety of expression possible in good writing, this text encourages individual students to experiment with the highly personal art of writing, and by doing so, to discover the art of putting words together, to discover the effectiveness of one combination rather than another, and to discover the challenge of writing with purpose—and the pleasure.

1

What is mature style?

Some thoughts about mature style

The problem of what constitutes a mature style may well escape solution. This chapter does not intend to solve the problem, but, rather, to set down some thoughts about recognizing mature and immature writing styles.

Can a person objectively determine the maturity of a prose style? Will the same standards apply to both fictional prose and expository prose? Can a person make an unbiased judgment as to whether or not his favorite writer has a mature style?

If such questions receive affirmative answers, then the criteria used to evaluate professional writers may help determine maturity, or lack of it, in students' writing, and, hopefully, will lead to a general improvement of student writing. Even if no such improvement occurs, the presentation of the material for consideration has merit, and one may draw upon that information at a later date.

Experts in composition have suggested several ways of determining mature style. To use any one of these methods, excluding the others, would probably result in unfair conclusions. This chapter will present four criteria of mature style with specific examples to illustrate each one, an entire fictional prose selection containing the examples used, and a chart presenting a compilation of statistics relative to this inquiry. This chart will allow the student to conduct his own investigations into the maturity of the style of two other prose selections presented at the end of the chapter.

To select at random one work of a writer and to judge him on the basis of that selection has its obvious dangers. Remember that the intended purpose of this chapter is to present several methods of evaluating the maturity of a writer's style, and that, ideally, any results should be further tested against other works by the same writers. However, in spite of these limitations, the selections provide much useful and interesting information.

The criteria

The first criterion, found in *The Perrin-Smith Handbook of Current English,* describes the relationship between grade levels and the *average number of words per sentence* used at each level. Commenting on writing development, the authors say, "In the early grades, pupils' sentences average 11 or 12 words; in high school, 17 to 19; in college, usually in the low 20's."

One factor that alters the average number of words per sentence in fictional prose appears in Ray Bradbury's "The Dragon." That factor, dialogue, makes up more than 50 percent of the last nine paragraphs of Bradbury's short story:

"Did you see it?" cried a voice. "Just like I told you!"

"The same! The same! A knight in armor, by the Lord Harry! We hit him!"

"You goin' to stop?"

"Did once; found nothing. Don't like to stop on this moor. I get the willies. Got a feel, it has."

"But we hit something!"

"Gave him plenty of whistle; chap wouldn't budge!"

A steaming blast cut the mist aside.

"We'll make Stokely on time. More coal, eh, Fred?"

Another whistle shook dew from the empty sky. The night train, in fire and fury, shot through a gully, up a rise, and vanished away over cold earth toward the north, leaving black smoke and steam to dissolve in the numbed air minutes after it had passed and gone forever.

These eighteen sentences contain 129 words and average 7.2 words per sentence, below the fourth-grade level according to Perrin's chart and below the early grade level according to Perrin and Smith's statement. Obviously such a statistic taken by itself would discredit Bradbury's writing ability. Therefore, one must always take into account, when gathering statistics, whether or not the passage of writing under examination contains dialogue. Referring again to the Bradbury selection, we notice that two of the nine paragraphs contain no dialogue. In the three sentences in these paragraphs, the author uses 57 words, an average of 19.0 words per sentence, considerably closer to the level normal for a college graduate or professional writer.

The second criterion, *variation* or *distribution*, depends on the ability to write long sentences. Dr. William Irmscher of the University of Washington has said, "The capacity to write a long sentence is a mark of a mature style." You will notice that Dr. Irmscher said "a mark," not "the mark"; in other words, this represents *one* indicator of mature style. That the mature writer is able to write the long sentence accounts for his high average of words per sentence, but, as with all such abilities, this one must be used thoughtfully. In testing for this ability, notice especially the writer's variation of sentence length. Does he use all short sentences? Does he mix the short and the long? Does he use all long sentences, which tend to create a very heavy, wordy style?

Consider two paragraphs, each with six sentences, whose pattern of variation looks like this:

PARAGRAPH A	PARAGRAPH B
12 words	16 words
18	20
20	19
40	21
20	18
6	22

Even though these figures represent hypothetical paragraphs, the average number of words per sentence and the variation in sentence length indicate a difference in writing abilities. Both paragraphs average 19.3 words per sentence, but paragraph A employs both the long and the short sentence. Paragraph B, while it has a twelfth-grade level of average number of words per sentence, has almost no variation in sentence length—a style difficult to read for very long. It makes little sense to label a style mature unless its creator has the ability to write and also to control long sentences.

Using Bradbury's short story again, we discover that its author can write both the short and the long sentence. At one point he writes this short, effective statement:

The two men froze.

Immediately following this he writes the following long, well-controlled sentence:

They waited a long time, but there was only the shake of their horses' nervous skin like black velvet tambourines jingling the silver stirrup buckles, softly, softly.

The final two criteria come from Francis Christensen's article, "The Problem of Defining a Mature Style," which appeared in the *English Journal*. Christensen defines *free modifiers*, the first of these criteria, as "... prepositional phrases; relative and subordinate clauses; noun, verb, adjective, and adverbial phrases or clusters; and, one of the most important, verbal clauses or absolutes." The use of free modifiers, usually set off by punctuation, appears at the beginning of independent clauses (initial), in the middle of independent clauses (medial), and at the end of independent clauses (final). However, the greatest number of these free modifiers appear in the final position.

FREE MODIFIER — INITIAL POSITION *prep. phrase 2*

Across the dim country, full of night and nothingness from the heart of the moor itself, the wind sprang full of dust from clocks that used dust for telling time.

FREE MODIFIER — MEDIAL POSITION

The midnight wilderness was split by a monstrous gushing as the dragon roared nearer, nearer; its flashing yellow glare spurted above a hill and then, *fold on fold of dark body, distantly seen, therefore indistinct,* flowed over that hill and plunged vanishing into a valley. *appositive (but poor)*

FREE MODIFIER — FINAL POSITION

participial phrase → The night train, in fire and fury, shot through a gully, up a rise, and vanished away over cold earth toward the north, *leaving black smoke and steam to dissolve in the numbed air minutes after it had passed and gone forever. infinitive phrase*
adverb clause

7

The paragraph below, again from Bradbury's short story, demonstrates the use of free modifiers and their positions in writing. (The free modifiers have been italicized for identification.)

> The lance struck under the unlidded yellow eye, buckled, tossed the man through the air. The dragon hit, spilled him over, *down*, ground him under. *Passing*, the black brunt of its shoulder smashing the remaining horse and rider a hundred feet against the side of a boulder, *wailing, wailing, the dragon shrieking, the fire all about, around, under it, a pink, yellow, orange sun-fire with great soft plumes of blinding smoke.*

This sample of 71 words has 26 words, or 37 percent of the paragraph, used as free modifiers, with one word in the initial position, one in the medial, and 24 in the final. Christensen's article says that a mature style has a high frequency of free modifiers; unfortunately, however, he does not define high frequency. Since over a third of this paragraph falls within the free modifier category, it seems fair to say that it has that high frequency and an especially high frequency (92 percent) of free modifiers in the final position.

Christensen's second criterion of mature style concerns "intra-T-unit coordination." A T-unit indicates an independent clause and its subordinate elements. *Intra-T-unit coordination* refers to structures of coordination within the independent clause, such as compounds linked by "and," coordinates linked by "or" and "and," or parallelisms linked by similar forms. A mature style, says Christensen, will have a high frequency of these intra-T-unit coordinations. But again he does not define high frequency.

Bradbury's short story helps us to see this criterion more clearly:

> In silence the men buckled on their armor and mounted their horses. The midnight wilderness was split by a monstrous gushing as the dragon roared nearer, nearer; its flashing yellow glare spurted above a hill and then, fold on fold of dark body, distantly seen, therefore indistinct, flowed over that hill and plunged vanishing into a valley.

Here we find a short paragraph with two sentences and three T-units, the second sentence being made up of two independent clauses or T-units. In each T-unit Bradbury used structures of coordination; the first contains "buckled . . . and mounted," the second "nearer, nearer," and the third "spurted . . . and . . . flowed . . . and plunged." Each represents intra-T-unit coordination, or some type of coordination within the independent clause.

The Dragon

RAY BRADBURY

The night blew in the short grass on the moor; there was no other motion. It had been years since a single bird had flown by in the great blind shell of sky. Long ago a few small stones had simulated life when they crumbled and fell into dust. Now only the night moved in the souls of the two men bent by their lonely fire in the wilderness; darkness pumped quietly in their veins and ticked silently in their temples and their wrists.

Firelight fled up and down their wild faces and welled in their eyes in orange tatters. They listened to each other's faint, cool breathing and the lizard blink of their eyelids. At last, one man poked the fire with his sword.

"Don't, idiot; you'll give us away!"

"No matter," said the second man. "The dragon can smell us miles off anyway. God's breath, it's cold. I wish I was back at the castle."

"It's death, not sleep, we're after. . . ."

"Why? Why? The dragon never sets foot in the town!"

"Quiet, fool! He eats men traveling alone from our town to the next!"

"Let them be eaten and let us get home!"

"Wait now; listen!"

The two men froze.

They waited a long time, but there was only the shake of their horses' nervous skin like black velvet tambourines jingling the silver stirrup buckles, softly, softly.

"Ah." The second man sighed. "What a land of nightmares. Everything happens here. Someone blows out the sun; it's night. And then, and then, oh, listen! This dragon, they say his eyes are fire. His breath a white gas; you can see him burn across the dark lands. He runs with sulfur and thunder and kindles the grass. Sheep panic and die insane. Women deliver forth monsters. The dragon's fury is such that tower walls shake back to dust. His victims, at sunrise, are strewn hither thither on the hills. How many knights, I ask, have gone for this monster and failed, even as we shall fail?"

"Enough of that!"

"More than enough! Out here in this desolation I cannot tell what year this is!"

"Nine hundred years since the Nativity."

"No, no," whispered the second man, eyes shut. "On this moor is no Time, is only Forever. I feel if I ran back on the road the town would be gone, the people yet unborn, things changed, the castles unquarried from the rocks, the timbers still uncut from the forests; don't ask how I know; the moor knows and tells me. And here we sit alone in the land of the fire dragon, God save us!"

"Be you afraid, then gird on your armor!"

"What use? The dragon runs from nowhere; we cannot guess its home. It vanishes in fog; we know not where it goes. Aye, on with our armor, we'll die well dressed."

Half into his silver corselet, the second man stopped again and turned his head.

Across the dim country, full of night and nothingness from the heart of the moor itself, the wind sprang full of dust from clocks that used dust for telling time. There were black suns burning in the heart of this new wind a million burnt leaves shaken from some autumn tree beyond the horizon. This wind melted landscapes, lengthened bones like white wax, made the blood roil and thicken to a muddy deposit in the brain. The wind was a thousand souls dying and all time confused and in transit. It was a fog inside of a mist inside of a darkness, and this place was no man's place and there was no year or hour at all, but only these men in a faceless emptiness of sudden frost, storm and white thunder which moved behind the great falling pane of green glass that was the lightning. A squall of rain drenched the turf; all faded away until there was unbreathing hush and the two men waiting alone with their warmth in a cool season.

"There," whispered the first man. "Oh, there . . ."

Miles off, rushing with a great chant and a roar—the dragon.

In silence the men buckled on their armor and mounted their horses. The midnight wilderness was split by a monstrous gushing as the dragon roared nearer, nearer; its flashing yellow glare spurted above a hill and then, fold on fold of dark body, distantly seen, therefore indistinct, flowed over that hill and plunged vanishing into a valley.

"Quick!"

They spurred their horses forward to a small hollow.

"This is where it passes!"

They seized their lances with mailed fists and blinded their horses by flipping the visors down over their eyes.

"Lord!"

"Yes, let us use His name."

On the instant, the dragon rounded a hill. Its monstrous amber eye fed on them, fired their armor in red glints and glitters. With a terrible wailing cry and a grinding rush it flung itself forward.

"Mercy!"

The lance struck under the unlidded yellow eye, buckled, tossed the man through the air. The dragon hit, spilled him over, down, ground him under. Passing, the black brunt of its shoulder smashing the remaining horse and rider a hundred feet against the side of a boulder, wailing, wailing, the dragon shrieking, the fire all about, around, under it, a pink, yellow, orange sun-fire with great soft plumes of blinding smoke.

"Did you see it?" cried a voice. "Just like I told you!"

"The same! The same! A knight in armor, by the Lord Harry! We hit him!"

"You goin' to stop?"

"Did once; found nothing. Don't like to stop on this moor. I get the willies. Got a feel, it has."

"But we hit something!"

"Gave him plenty of whistle; chap wouldn't budge!"

A steaming blast cut the mist aside.

"We'll make Stokely on time. More coal, eh, Fred?"

Another whistle shook dew from the empty sky. The night —train, in fire and fury, shot through a gully, up a rise, and vanished away over cold earth toward the north, leaving black smoke and steam to dissolve in the numbed air minutes after it had passed and gone forever.

Application of criteria

Having looked at the several criteria for mature style, we may now apply these principles to the entire Bradbury short story, remembering, in this case, to compile statistics two ways, with and without the dialogue. The chart below will serve as an example of how to compile and to organize the necessary statistics.

Note: Under the second criterion, variation in sentence length, the chart gives the statistics relating to the variation of sentence length, the number of long sentences, and the percentage of long sentences in relation to the total number of sentences. Under the third criterion, frequency of free modifiers, the chart gives the percentage of the total word count used as free modifiers and also the percentage of free modifiers in the final position.

The Dragon — Ray Bradbury

CRITERIA	WITH DIALOGUE	WITHOUT DIALOGUE
Average number of words per sentence	10.9	20.2
Variation in sentence length		
(a) spread	1 to 57	4 to 57
(b) number of long sentences	11	10
(c) percentage of long sentences	12	33⅓
Frequency of free modifiers		
(a) percentage of total	15	17
(b) percentage of final position	51	51
Frequency of intra-T-unit coordination (percentage of T-units with coordination)	28	64

ADDITIONAL PROSE MODELS FOR INVESTIGATION

Remarks on Receiving the Nobel Prize

WILLIAM FAULKNER

I feel that this award was not made to me as a man but to my work—a life's work in the agony and sweat of the human spirit, not for glory and least of all for profit, but to create out of the materials of the human spirit something which did not exist before. So this award is only mine in trust. It will not be difficult to find a dedication for the money part of it commensurate with the purpose and significance of its origin. But I would like to do the same with the acclaim too, by using this moment as a pinnacle from which I might be listened to by the young men and women already dedicated to the same anguish and travail, among whom is already that one who will some day stand here where I am standing.

Our tragedy today is a general and universal physical fear so long sustained by now that we can even bear it. There are no longer problems of the spirit. There is only the question: when will I be blown up? Because of this, the young man or woman writing today has forgotten the problems of the human heart in conflict with itself which alone can make good writing because only that is worth writing about, worth the agony and sweat.

He must learn them again. He must teach himself that the basest of all things is to be afraid; and, teaching himself that, forget it forever, leaving no room in his workshop for anything but the old verities and truths of the heart, the old universal truths lacking which any story is ephemeral and doomed—love and honor and pity and pride and compassion and sacrifice. Until he does so he labors under a curse. He writes not of love but of lust, of defeats in which nobody loses anything of value, of victories without hope, and worst of all, without pity or compassion. His griefs grieve on no universal bones, leaving no scars. He writes not of the heart but of the glands.

Until he relearns these things he will write as though he stood alone and watched the end of man. I decline to accept the end of man. It is easy enough to say that man is immortal simply because he will endure; that when the last ding-dong of doom has clanged and faded from the last worthless rock hanging tideless in the last red and dying evening, that even then there will still be one more sound: that of his puny inexhaustible voice, still talking. I refuse to accept this. I believe that man will not merely endure: he will prevail. He is immortal, not because he alone among creatures has an inexhaustible voice, but because he has a soul, a spirit capable of compassion and sacrifice and endurance. The poet's, the writer's, duty is to write about these things. It is his privilege to help man endure by lifting his heart, by reminding him of the courage and honor and hope and pride and compassion and pity and sacrifice which have been the glory of his past. The poet's voice need not merely be the record of man, it can be one of the props, the pillars to help him endure and prevail.

Application of criteria

Using the chart presented earlier in this chapter as a model, construct another chart incorporating statistics for the Faulkner selection.

Fantastic Journey

HOLLIS ALPERT

Now and then a movie project gets started that involves its makers in a greater outlay of time and energy than was at first envisaged; when the result finally emerges on the screen there is invariably the tendency to wonder if the effort was justified. I suspect this is going to happen in the case of Stanley Kubrick's *2001: A Space Odyssey*. Kubrick's last film was the mordant and provoking *Dr. Strangelove*, released in 1964. We can assume that since then this youngish and remarkably gifted film-maker has been engaged on his cinematic visualization of the first human encounter with what sci-fi writers and addicts call extra-terrestrial intelligence, and which some believers in flying saucers and related "sightings" regard firmly as reality.

Kubrick really isn't that type, however. He is obviously fascinated by current space hardware and projections of future developments in the field. He is also aware of the mathematical possibilities in favor of the supposition that some form of intelligent life exists elsewhere in the charted and uncharted reaches of the universe. And he is far too clever to couch his fantasy in the clichéd terms of Hollywood science-fiction: monsters, and "things" of one horrible kind or another. He has also had the collaboration of one of the most intelligent writers of science-fiction and science-fact, Arthur

C. Clarke. Between them they first drafted a novel (based on a Clarke short story) detailing the kind of space adventure Kubrick had in mind for his film, and from this built the screenplay—which, by the way, has been kept under wraps during the long period of production.

An important part of Kubrick's plan was to develop new and improved special-effects techniques that would create the illusion of flight in space and that would give audiences the realistic feel of exploring our solar system. A space station, a huge double wheel, revolves at a calculated speed in space to give its occupants a gravitational weight similar to their accustomed one on earth. A space shuttle, run by that familiar firm, Pan American, carries its lone and important passenger to the station, and another vehicle takes him the rest of the way to a landing in an underground moon base. This kind of thing is beautiful, even breathtaking to watch, and somehow Kubrick's choice of an old-fashioned waltz, *The Blue Danube,* to accompany the space acrobatics gives the right sense of innocent, almost naive scientific adventure that is part of the story scheme at this point.

There is no doubt at all that Kubrick has notably advanced film technique when it comes to achieving perspective for this kind of trickery; how he has done it as yet remains a mystery. Also, for an early section of the film called "The Dawn of Man," he found a way through the use of special lenses, transparencies, and mirrored screens, to enact on a soundstage scenes that would have otherwise required a long location sojourn in some desolate place of the world. Conceivably, if other directors are allowed to make use of similar methods, some of the more difficult kinds of location work can be drastically lessened or eliminated altogether—a development many in Hollywood would welcome.

But Kubrick and Clarke had more than mere space adventure in mind. They were concerned with the physical and metaphysical implications of an encounter with some otherworldly form of intelligence, if such were ever to occur. They have certainly been bold and imaginative—more so than any others who have played with the prospect in the film medium—but, as shown on the giant Cinerama screen, the awaited spectacle does come as something of a letdown. Somehow we had expected more than we get, and, at the same time, Kubrick puzzles us both by what he does present and how he presents it.

Intriguing indeed is the use of a monolith—a large slab—as the symbol of an extraterrestrial presence and the key to the story. The slab first appears before a colony of apelike creatures and becomes a sort of "gate" to the knowledge that will allow the development of man as we know him. In essence, the primitive grubbers discover how to make use of a weapon and become carnivorous and thus take the first step toward developing the ability to reach the moon some 4,000,000 years later. Time: 2001 A.D., and now another slab, 4,000,000 years old, is found buried beneath the moon's surface—as though someone or something out there knew this would happen. The slab emits an ear-splitting signal which is tracked to the vicinity of Jupiter. Eventually (some two hours of film time later), a third slab is encountered by the lone surviving occupant of a spaceship about to orbit the distant planet. What happens next might cause some moviegoers to wonder if a solution of LSD has been wafted through the air-conditioning system, for the astronaut now, presumably, enters unknown dimensions of time and space not unlike a psychedelic tunnel in the heavens, and lands in—of all possible places—a kind of translucent Louis Seize apartment.

The fourth slab appears before the aged astronaut as he lies dying in his splendid isolation, after which, in embryonic form, he floats back through space to twenty-first-century earth and whatever destiny the viewer might want to imagine. It is this weirdly far-out finale that has a way of putting a strain on the longest section of the film—that dealing with the long Jupiter trip. Aboard are two active astronauts, three others in "hibernaculums" and an advanced computer that has been programed with human feelings and emotions. Hal, the computer, is there for company and control of the functions of the spacecraft. When Hal begins to make mistakes as "he" puts it, matters get pretty sticky for Gary Lockwood and Keir Dullea, the two non-hibernating astronauts.

And for the audience, too. Kubrick seems much too fascinated with his intricate and scrupulously detailed, even scientifically plausible space hardware. Those who dote on that sort of thing are going to share Kubrick's fascination. Others are going to wish for speedier space travel. Then, too, this almost mundanely technical section is poles apart from the wide-ranging fantastics of the final episodes. And for all the beautiful models, the marvelous constructions, the sensational perspectives, the effort to equate scientific accuracy with imaginative projections, there is gnawing lack of some genuinely human contact with the participants in the adventure. In fact, most human of all is Hal, the computer, and we feel more concerned with the electronic lobotomy performed on him than with anything that happens to the living and breathing actors. With all the sweep and spectacle, there is a pervading aridity. If people are going to behave like automatons, what happens to them isn't going to matter much, even if they become privy to metaphysical secrets.

Nevertheless, Kubrick has, in one big jump, discovered new possibilities for the screen image. He took on a large challenge, and has met it commendably. One quibble, though. There are still problems of distortion in that curving Cinerama screen—not of great concern when things are moving fast, but, on the longer takes, definitely an annoyance. Too bad Kubrick didn't overhaul the Cinerama system while tinkering with everything else.

Application of criteria

Using the chart presented earlier in this chapter as a model, construct a chart showing the statistics relating to the Alpert selection.

Conclusions

Though limited, the statistics gathered here may have something to say about a mature prose style. What do we discover about the following?

a. the effect of dialogue on a writer's average number of words per sentence
b. a comparative analysis, using Perrin's chart of the Bradbury, Faulkner, and Alpert pieces
c. the ability of these writers to deal with long sentences
d. the use of free modifiers, both overall and in the final position
e. the use of intra-T-unit coordination

2

Syntax as a factor in style

Introduction

In our study of grammar in earlier years, we learned the structural elements of the simple sentence, the compound sentence, and the complex sentence. We learned that single words, phrases, or clauses can modify nouns or verbs. We learned that *subject-verb-object* represents the common word order in English and that syntax (the arrangement of words in a sentence to show their relationship) invariably carries much of the meaning in any sentence. Syntax, of course, depends greatly on a writer's style. For, although not all modifiers have a movable quality, the writer usually has many options as to the placement of modifiers. Modifiers of nouns must usually come next to the noun or noun cluster modified, for reasons of clarity. Those embedded immovably in a main clause we call *bound modifiers.* Modifiers of the whole sentence or modifiers set off with some mark of punctuation always can be moved; we call them *free modifiers*. As pointed out in Chapter One, these free modifier structures include prepositional phrases, dependent clauses, noun, verbal, adjectival, and adverbial phrases, as well as absolutes.

To analyze a writer's style—and to improve one's own—we should review some of the syntactic structures that, with expert use, can give variety to a writer's style. Mastering the use of these structures develops maturity in composition. The following lessons will review some common syntactic structures that can affect style.

Begin with expansion drill – add constructions & complexity

Lesson one — the appositive

One of the simplest syntactic devices for achieving economy in writing is the appositive. *An appositive represents a word or group of words that closely follows a noun or pronoun and identifies or explains it.*

How does the appositive save words? For example, one might say:

She brought her friend to the meeting. Dominic is her friend.

But one could say with greater economy:

She brought her friend *Dominic* to the meeting.

The example above illustrates a single word serving as an appositive. A series of nouns, a noun clause, or a noun modified by a phrase or by an adjective clause can also serve as an appositive. How many words do we save by this change? Does the meaning change in any way?

SERIES OF NOUNS *(single word(s))*

At noon he delivered the groceries—*potatoes, cereals, bread, cheese, and milk.*

NOUN CLAUSE

Her story—*that she had missed her train*—did not impress her father.

NOUN WITH MODIFYING PHRASE

Jonathan, *a young student of architecture*, won an award for creative design.

NOUN WITH MODIFYING CLAUSE

The abandoned building, *a brownstone that had seen better days*, has been sold for taxes.

Appositives add information to sentences by specifying or expanding some noun or pronoun. For writers, these structures present an effective means of achieving not only economy and conciseness, but also clarity, concreteness, variety, and emphasis.

Normally, an appositive follows the term it renames or explains. An appositive can precede the term if the writer deliberately shifts its position for effect.

SHIFTED POSITION

A brownstone that had seen better days, the abandoned building has been sold for taxes.

Shifting the position of an appositive may lead to confusion unless one places it closer to the noun to which it refers than to any other noun. An even worse situation can occur if a writer omits entirely the noun to which the appositive refers.

MISPLACED APPOSITIVE

 A novel of unusual quality, the critic will interview the author of *Herzog.* *(a novel of unusual quality.)*

DANGLING APPOSITIVE

 A young man of twenty-three, Jack's long drives amaze golf professionals.

What problems arise in the two examples above? How would one remedy each situation?

Exercise in analysis

Below, you will find seven passages from works of professional writers. (This does not include the passage in the composition exercise.) For each, including those passages containing more than one appositive, we can now identify the following:

a. each entire appositive construction
b. the word or words to which each appositive refers

(1) Most important of all, they have helped build many great names of American industry: Coca-Cola, General Motors, Wrigley, Standard Oil, Ford, and many others.
—Harley B. Markham, "What's the Shouting About?"

medial

(2) All those letters—George's letters and John's letters and her letters to them both—lying around for the children to find afterwards made her uneasy.

—Katherine Anne Porter, "The Jilting of Granny Weatherall"

final
medial

(3) One winter, years ago, I lived in a house on the road to Santa Monica. Less than a mile away, in an open California field, lay the tar pits of Rancho La Brea, the so-called Death Trap of the Ages. The great beasts of the earth—the saber-toothed tiger, the dire wolf, the imperial elephant—had been caught there like insects on flypaper.

—Edwin Way Teale, "Winged Bullets"

final

(4) The river lay in this direction; near its bank stood a grove of fruit trees—peach, pear, cherry, and apple.

—Truman Capote, In Cold Blood

final

(5) Occupying the Empire bedroom and Georgian suites of the first-class accommodations were many well-known men and women—Colonel John Jacob Astor and his young bride; Major Archibald Butt, military aid to President Taft, and his friend, Frank D. Millet, the painter; John B. Thayer, vice-president of the Pennsylvania Railroad, and Charles M. Hays, president of the Grand Trunk Railway of Canada; W. T. Stead, the English journalist; Jacques Futrelle, French novelist; H. B. Harris, theatrical manager, and Mrs. Harris; Mr. and Mrs. Isidor Straus; and J. Bruce Ismay, chairman and managing director of the White Star Line.

—Hanson W. Baldwin, "R.M.S. Titanic"

initial

(6) Some sprained shoulders, wrists, and ankles; livid contusions; wrenched harpoons and lances; inextricable intricacies of rope; shattered oars and planks; all these were there; but no fatal or even serious ill seemed to have befallen any one.

—Herman Melville, Moby Dick

initial

(7) The needy and adventurous, the gambling speculator, the dreaming land jobber, the thriftless tradesman, the merchant with cracked credit—in short, everyone driven to raise money by desperate means and desperate sacrifices hurried to Tom Walker.

—Washington Irving, "The Devil and Tom Walker"

21

Exercise in composition

Dog owners spent $530 million on dog food last year, reports the Wall Street Journal, which adds that this is about 50 percent more than Americans spend on baby food! But there's more: Americans will spend $1.5 billion to acquire pets this year and in addition to the initial investment and the food bill, about $800 million will be spent this year on non-food items for pets. (For dogs: pajamas, cashmere sweaters, mink collars, Halloween costumes and Santa Claus suits; and cosmetics—color shampoo, creme rinses and hair dressing, perfumes, eleven shades of nail polish including lavender and green, a spray dentifrice, tranquilizers, etc.) Not to mention the millions spent on veterinarian fees and boarding kennels. Pets are big business!

—Charles A. Wells,
"Some Questions of Values"

After reading the Wells selection, construct a paragraph in reaction to this information. Make use of at least one appositive construction.

Lesson two — the working verb

Writers, especially inexperienced ones, can easily and unconsciously develop the habit of laziness, a habit out of place in good writing. To write creatively and effectively and to improve our use of syntactic structures, we must avoid lazy habits, especially the overuse of any one particular device or structure.

The lazy writer and the fuzzy thinker mistreat the "be" verbs—*is, are, was, were, be, am,* and *been.* These "be" verbs have a static nature, giving no feeling of forward movement.

WEAK VERB

The students' uncompromising behavior was the subject of Mrs. Smith's complaint.

STRONGER VERB

Mrs. Smith complained about the students' uncompromising behavior.

Fuzzy thinkers construct vague sentences by relying on "be." This reliance encourages the use of wordy and unnecessary phrases, or indirect and inconcise phrases, which add nothing to the meaning and in fact reduce any impact the sentence might have had.

WEAK VERB AND WORDINESS

Structural faults in the freeway were the cause of the closing of two traffic lanes.

STRONGER VERB AND CONCISENESS

Structural faults in the freeway caused the closure of two traffic lanes.

Likewise, the lazy writer-thinker will mistreat the impersonal and usually vague "there is," "there are," and "it is" constructions. These tend to weaken writing. A word like "there" usually contributes only clutter and, as a result, drains the vitality from a sentence. *Expletive Constructions*

WEAK "IT IS" CONSTRUCTION

It is the opinion of the author of *The Red Badge of Courage* that Henry Fleming never achieves courage.

CLUTTER ELIMINATED

The author of *The Red Badge of Courage* believes Henry Fleming never achieves courage.

Instead of being satisfied with weak verb constructions, writers should put a strong, more specific verb to work. They should search the sentence for a potential verb and convert it into the sentence's dominant verb, or eliminate bland structures completely and reconstruct the sentence with an entirely new subject and verb.

Generally, writers should avoid lazy verbs and actively search out verbs that will work for them. But that writers should avoid completely the use of the verb "to be," as has been seriously suggested by people who should know better, borders on the ridiculous and the impossible. Therefore, its use needs to be kept in proper perspective; it does serve at least two valuable purposes.

EFFECTIVE USES OF "BE" VERB

1. To describe a condition or a predicament:

   Man is totally depraved!

   I have never been in such a situation.

   It was the coldest day in years.

   It's raining!

2. To add effect to many colloquial or idiomatic expressions:

   It's the greatest!

   That's true.

   You're nuts.

The weak "be" verbs also contribute to the problems of passive voice. When we speak of *voice*, we mean *that property of a verb which indicates whether the subject of the verb acts or is acted upon. In active voice the subject acts; somebody (or something) does something. In passive voice the subject does not act, rather someone or something acts upon it; the passive contains some form of the verb "be" plus the past participle.*

ACTIVE VOICE

On the 4th of July, firecrackers exploded, roman candles flung color into the blackness, and sparklers fluttered and flickered in the distance.

PASSIVE VOICE

On the 4th of July, firecrackers (were exploded) color (was flung) into the blackness by roman candles, and in the distance the fluttering and flickering of sparklers (could be seen)

Active voice tends to produce fresh, strong, direct writing; passive voice tends to produce stale, weak, indirect writing. And, since the passive suggests an unknown or a relatively anonymous doer of an action, its frequent use weakens writing because of its vagueness and wordiness.

Exercise in rewriting

In certain types of writing, such as the minutes of meetings and some newspaper reporting, we have used the passive voice for so long that we now accept this style of writing in those cases. The names of persons in the following article have been changed.

Mrs. Jane Doe, 56, who was admitted to Western State Hospital last year following her acquittal on a charge of strangling her husband, was reported missing from the institution yesterday.

A spokesman for the hospital said Mrs. Doe went "on unauthorized leave" June 27. She was in a rehabilitation ward where patients are free to come and go.

Mrs. Doe was found not guilty of second-degree murder by a King County jury in October of 1967. The jury found she was insane at the time of the crime but not at the time of her trial.

However, the jury decided there was a possibility of a recurrence of the insanity and it was unsafe for her to be at large. Subsequently, she was sent to Western State Hospital.

Her estranged husband, John, also 56, was found dead in her Seattle apartment July 5, 1967.

Seattle Post-Intelligencer

The instances of passive voice and uses of "be" verbs fail to give a vigorous style to the article. Rewrite the article in a more direct, more concise manner.

The anonymous quality of passive voice, its greatest weakness, stems from the fact that the passive tends to eliminate from the sentence anyone who acts, creating the effect of a ghostly nobody doing something. But, by using the active, we can eliminate the anonymous voice and the superfluous prepositional phrase. (stating the doer)

However, the elimination of the passive by changing the sentence's subject has its limitations. This sentence illustrates the problem: *change to active voice — retain lightning as subject — working verbs*

Lightning was seen in the dark southern sky.

Apparently the sentence above means something like this:

Several persons saw lightning in the dark southern sky.

or

People saw lightning in the dark southern sky.

But, rather than being tied to sentences as colorless as these, why not use a subject that asserts itself, one that has a person or thing doing something definite?

Lightning split the dark southern sky.

or

Lightning illuminated the dark southern sky.

or

Lightning sliced through the dark southern sky.

If the subject performs, then we must have action—motion and vitality—and active, working verbs transmit this. One might say:

The window (was blown) shut with a bang.

But, if we put the verb to work, we could have a sentence like:

The window banged shut.

By avoiding limp passive constructions and by concentrating on the stronger active ones, we can create verbal pictures that capture all the vitality of the original scene. The following progression illustrates how the substitution of an active verb for the passive can produce a more vivid image for the reader, an image that changes with each new variation of the verb:

A man (could be seen) walking down the street. *Passive Voice*

A man (walked) down the street. *Active Voice — flat verb*

or

A man strolled down the street. *Active Voice — Working Verbs*

or

A man plodded down the street.

or

A man staggered down the street.

or

A man waddled down the street.

Exercise in composition

In the paragraph below, the verbs and their effect color the sentences and the paragraph as a whole. Rewrite the paragraph, eliminating every passive construction and redesigning or combining any of the sentences where you think it necessary. *Underline the strong, active verbs you substitute for the weak, passive verbs in the paragraph.*

26

A man was seen at an intersection, calmly crossing against the light. Cars were brought to a shrieking halt. Horns were honked. Warnings were shouted by a crowd waiting on the corner, and in the distance a series of small crashes could be heard from the growing line of cars as bumpers were engaged unexpectedly. None of this was noticed by the man, a narrow-chested little fellow in a black suit. A black briefcase was carried in one hand and a rolled umbrella in the other. When the opposite side of the intersection was reached, his umbrella was raised in a brief salute to the cars that were now hopelessly stalled for blocks because of him. Then he was seen no more.

—Lucile Vaughan Payne, *The Lively Art of Writing*

Lesson three —
the participial construction

To subordinate ideas or to combine sentences, a writer may often reduce a sentence to a phrase. The verbal phrases represent one way of doing this. The term verbal *designating a word derived from a verb, but not itself a verb,* covers three classifications—participles, gerunds, and infinitives—each of the three being part verb and part something else.

The participle one of the most frequently used syntactic structures, *shares qualities that mark verbs and adjectives.* Like a verb, it may take an object; like an adjective, it modifies a noun or pronoun. To help clarify this dual nature, we can graphically illustrate the participle's overlapping roles by using the following diagram:

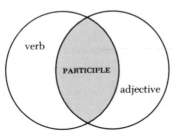

Many participles, but not all of them, end in *-ing, -ed,* or *d.*

Participial phrases effectively convey information that the writer wants closely linked to the modified noun, but that, at the same time, he wants clearly subordinated to the sentence's main idea. For example, one might write:

I saw their car drive in. I ran to greet our guests.
main idea
(economy)

Through the use of a participial phrase, however, we can combine these two jerky sentences into a single fluid one:

Seeing their car drive in, I ran to greet our guests.
(subordinate)

Many writers use the verb quality of the participle in description. Combining description and suggesting motion, participles help create a sense of life and activity, as this sentence illustrates:

The mothers stayed back in the kitchen *washing and drying, putting* things away, *recrossing* their traceless footsteps like the lifetime journeys of bees, *measuring* out the dry cocoa for breakfast.

—James Agee, *A Death in the Family*

Because participles should refer clearly to the noun or pronoun modified, the placement of participles becomes important not only for sentence strength but also for sentence sense. In the following sentence the compound participles immediately precede the pronoun "he" that they modify:

Worn and ragged, he collapsed on the park bench.

Participles placed improperly or constructed improperly create structures that, when analyzed, do not make sense. The term *dangling participles* aptly describes them.

IMPROPERLY PLACED PARTICIPLE   *(wrong word modified)*
Hanging from the ceiling, I saw an enormous cobweb.

IMPROPERLY CONSTRUCTED PARTICIPLE

Driving down the street, the beautiful cathedral seemed very large.   *(dangling — no word modified)*

What problem does each example have? How would one eliminate the problems in each sentence?

Exercise in analysis

The six passages below (including the model from Nathanson in the composition exercise) contain participial constructions. In the following passages, find:

a. each participle or participial phrase
b. the word or words to which each participle refers

initial
medial
(1) Looking upwards, a furze-cutter would have been inclined to continue work; looking down, he would have decided to finish his faggot and go home.

—Thomas Hardy, *The Return of the Native*

medial
(2) They flew past Tonio Kroger to a maddeningly quick tempo, crossing, advancing, retreating, with quick, breathless laughter.

—Thomas Mann, "Tonio Kroger"

initial
(3) Panting and worn out, with a yellowed sprig of basil behind one ear and cigarette behind the other, the brother stood on the threshold, his woolen cloak thrown round his shoulders.

—Nikos Kazantzakis, *Freedom or Death*

initial
medial
(4) Moving through the air high spars of a three-master, her sails brailed up on the crosstrees, homing upstream, silently moving, a silent ship.

—James Joyce, *Ulysses*

medial
(5) Two men waited beside the mules; the guide was adjusting a stirrup and beside him, scratching under the armpit, awaiting his coming with a doubtful and defensive smile, stood the half-caste. *gerund*

—Graham Greene, *The Power and the Glory*

Exercise in composition

Odell heard the words, saw the figures moving one hundred feet below him, heard the rattling explosions, and with fascinated disbelief watched the bullets chewing into the cliff, spitting out bits of sandstone as the stream moved upward toward his perch—and he jumped! his hands and arms and legs enmeshed with the rope, flying upward out of the welling of noise and dust and exploding rock with a new kind of fear that galvanized him scurrying past the overhang as though it wasn't there—nobody helping him because they'd all jumped back from the chattering gun!— and he dropped trembling and exultant beside the bug-eyed prisoners on the plateau. He had done it! He had done it, and more! Fired upon! He! Tasted what surely was heat of battle! Felt tiny shards of death speed past and leave him unscathed! Oh God, he'd showed them!

—E. M. Nathanson, The Dirty Dozen

The paragraph above illustrates the great contribution of the participle to the description of action. This paragraph contains at least a dozen participles, but <u>no passive voice</u>, and only one "be" verb.

Expanding the following notes or ideas, write a paragraph that combines description, action, and the use of the participial structure: *Underline participles + participial phrase*

A quiet town. Night. Silence broken by an alarm. People run into the darkness. Some make it. Some don't.

Lesson four — the gerund construction

The *gerund* may function as either a <u>noun</u> or as a <u>verb</u> in a sentence. As a noun the gerund displays exactly those characteristics common to the noun, namely, the ability to function as subject, direct object, indirect object, predicate noun, object of a preposition or appositive. The (*-ing* ending) the ability to take an object, and the dependence of adjective or adverb (modifiers) characterize the verbal nature of the gerund. The diagram below illustrates the dual nature of the gerund:

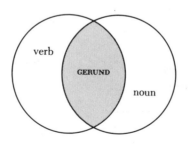

The following examples illustrate the gerund functioning as a noun:

SUBJECT (Obj.)

[Being] a good student involves discipline and hard work.

DIRECT OBJECT (Mod.)

Bob tried [running] to improve his health.

INDIRECT OBJECT (Obj.)

Dave gave [selling] newspapers the credit for developing his sense about the worth of money.

PREDICATE NOMINATIVE (Obj.) (Mod.)

Her hobby is [collecting] dolls from countries all over the world.

OBJECT OF A PREPOSITION (Obj.)

After [winning] the game, the victor addressed the fans.

APPOSITIVE

Ron worked his way through college with his special talent, [photographing] campus life.

We sometimes confuse gerunds and participles. A gerund in one sentence may act as a participle in another. How does the word "dancing" function in these two sentences?

Her [dancing] continues to be very impressive.   Gerund as Subject

I could not afford [dancing] lessons.   Participle modifying lessons

Like other verbals, gerunds can combine related thoughts and add compactness to a sentence. Their use can tighten a piece of writing by converting an idea contained in a weak compound sentence into a more streamlined gerund phrase. For example, this sentence:

The Wilson High School Tigers lost; they had won seven games in a row.

Converting the second clause into a gerund phrase produces this result:

31

The Wilson High School Tigers lost *after winning seven* *(Obj. Prep.)* *(Obj.)*
games in a row.

Gerund phrases do not necessarily have to replace subordinate *(Obj.) (Mod.)*
clauses. In some cases, we must use subordinate clauses to make
a relationship between ideas clearer.

Relating the gerund phrase to parts of the sentence other
than those it properly modifies results in a *dangling gerund*.

DANGLING GERUND

By going out into the country, the river will be seen. ?

What needs to be done to correctly reconstruct the above
sentence?

Adjectives that precede and modify gerunds use the posses-
sive form:

Hamlet's babbling frightened Ophelia.

John's father objects to *John's* having the car tonight. *(Obj.) (Mod.)*

What reasons do you have for *your* always being late? *(Mod.)*

Exercise in analysis

The seven passages below, from works of professional writers,
have gerunds. (This includes the model from Brodkey in the
composition exercise.) In each passage:

a. identify each gerund or gerund phrase
b. tell how each gerund functions in the sentence

present prog. tense (1) This problem of a loophole obsesses me; I am always *aux* (*part.*) wondering if there have been cases of condemned prisoners' *(Part.)* *compound* escaping from the implacable machinery of justice at the *Mod. ger.* *object* last moment, breaking through the police cordon, vanishing *of* in the nick of time before the guillotine falls. *preposition* *(Mod. ger.)*
—Albert Camus, *The Stranger*

(Obj. Prep.) (Obj. Ger.) (2) She walked in the moonlight without seeing it, past the frogs in the bulrushes without hearing them; through the moist woods without smelling them. *Prep.) (Obj.) ger.*
(Obj. Prep.) —Ellen Glasgow, *Barren Ground* *(Obj. ger.)*

32

(3) In the first place, it means buying a boat, then finding some place to keep the thing, then finding someone to explain the difference between tacking and keelhauling.

—Russell Baker, "The Paradox of the New Leisure"

(4) When, after one of these Saturdays spent in housecleaning, baking, washing and ironing, after milking and feeding the cow, my grandmother immersed herself from top to toe in the tub, when after leaving a little of herself in the soapsuds and letting the water in the tub sink back to its normal level, she sat down on the edge of the bed swathed in a great flowery towel, the four worn skirts and the freshly washed skirt lay spread out before her on the floor.

—Günter Grass, *The Tin Drum*

(5) Mary lived in a feeling of nightmare, writing letters, mimeographing appeals, making speeches at meetings of clothing and fur workers, canvassing wealthy liberals.

—John Dos Passos, *The Big Money*

(6) That was the kind of office life she was used to, making coffee, buying cakes, and being told stories with a proper beginning and end.

—Heinrich Böll, *Billiards at Half-Past Nine*

Exercise in composition

"There's some soup," my mother said. "Why don't I heat it up." And suddenly her eyes filled with tears, and all at once we fell to kissing one another—to embracing and smiling and making cheerful predictions about one another—there in the white, brightly lighted kitchen. We had known each other for so long, and there were so many things that we all three remembered.... Our smiles, our approving glances, wandered from face to face. There was a feeling of politeness in the air. We were behaving the way we would in railway stations, at my sister's wedding, at the birth of her first child, at my graduation from college. This was the first of our reunions.

—Harold Brodkey, "First Love and Other Sorrows"

This effectively written paragraph—last in a short story of a high school boy's remembrances—impresses because of its use

33

of gerunds, balanced construction, and varying sentence lengths. The statistics below show the range in length of the author's sentences in this one paragraph:

SENTENCE	NUMBER OF WORDS
1	6
2	6
3	35
4	19
5	10
6	9
7	26
8	7

The author not only writes both short and long sentences, but also strategically places the short sentences to produce the effect he wants. For example, look at the seven-word last sentence.

By using gerunds and by varying sentence length (with special care devoted to the short ones), expand the information that follows into a paragraph. Supply both description and an ending from your own imagination:

A man lying on a narrow ledge on the face of a mountain. Darkness. Icy winds. Bitter cold. Pain and cold cut into the man's body. A noise just above him in the darkness. Then . . .

This exercise calls for concentration on the man and his immediate situation. You need not worry about how he happened to get into this predicament or what he does with the rest of his life.

Lesson five — the infinitive structure

This syntactic structure has more functions than the participle or the gerund. Where the participle serves only as an adjective and the gerund only as a noun, the *infinitive* may serve as a noun, adjective, or adverb. The three diagrams and the three models will illustrate the overlapping roles of the infinitive:

NOUN

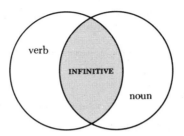

Subject

To feel *that Mrs. Bowen has been overly optimistic is not* to accept *the dark view of old age held by the author of* Ecclesiastes.... *Predicate Nominative*
—Elmer Davis, "Grandeurs and Miseries of Old Age"

ADJECTIVE

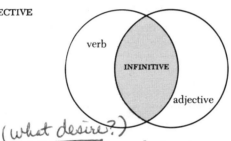

(what desire?)

This desire to please ... graduates at one end of the scale into a general kindliness, into public benefactions, hospitals, and college foundations; at the other end it is seen melting into a desire to efface *rather than* give *offense,* to hide *rather than* be noticed.

—John Jay Chapman, "Society"

ADVERB

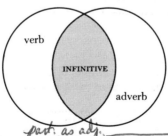

past as adj.

Yet the testimony is too amusing to be neglected *and some of it is far too important* to be ignored.

(adj) —Bliss Perry, "The American Mind"

35

Another characteristic distinguishes the infinitive from the other verbals. The infinitive usually contains *to,* the sign of the infinitive. But this sign can often cause trouble. It is possible to confuse this *to* with the preposition *to.* In the following sentences, (for example), "to" functions as a preposition:

He went *to* dancing school.

His summer was given to sailing.

Sometimes we omit the sign of the infinitive. We may safely leave it out when its presence is understood, as in the following sentences:

Please help us win the prize.

I have never seen the Giants play.

He would not dare tell a lie.

Writers can also misconstruct, and therefore misuse, the infinitive structure. One must be aware of exactly what the infinitive in any sentence modifies, and whether such modification can exist and, therefore, make sense.

DANGLING INFINITIVES

To understand the writings of James Joyce, many things must be known about Ireland.

To excel in any sport, tremendous dedication is necessary.

What problems do these sentences have? How would one eliminate the difficulties?

Too often writers, and especially students, have been chastised for the *splitting of infinitives,* that is, the placing of some modifier or modifiers between *to,* the sign of the infinitive, and the verbal itself. Instead of complete condemnation of this practice, a wiser course might be to avoid the split infinitive when it sounds awkward. For example, "He wanted to very quickly go" sounds lumpy; "He wanted to go very quickly" has a much better effect.

There are, then, exceptions to the old rule. A sentence beginning "I want it to be fully understood that ..." sounds better than any of the following:

I want it to be understood fully that ...

I want it fully to be understood that ...

36

And, similarly, why not use a phrase like "to carefully assemble"? Thus, situations occur when to split an infinitive becomes not only acceptable but desirable. *Not proven.*

Exercise in analysis

The seven passages below (including the student writing in the composition exercise) contain infinitive structures. For every example, determine the following:

a. each infinitive phrase
b. how each infinitive functions (noun, adjective, or adverb)
c. what each infinitive modifies *Vs specific*

passive voice

(1) But to be stopped on the stairs, to be forced to listen to her trivial, irrelevant gossip, (to (pestering) demands for payment, threats and complaints, and to rack his brains for excuses, to prevaricate, to lie—no, rather than that, he would creep down the stairs like a cat and slip out unseen.
—Fyodor Dostoyevsky, *Crime and Punishment*

(2) To roam the roads of the country or the streets of the city, to feel there is no rood of ground on which the feet can rest, to halt weary and hungry outside lighted windows and (to) hear laughter and song within—these are the hungers and rebellions that drive men to crime and women to shame.
—Hamlin Garland, "Under the Lion's Paw"

(3) The truth was, the nation as a body was in the world for one object, and one only: to grovel before the king and Church and noble; to slave for them, sweat blood for them, to starve that they might be fed, work that they might play, to drink misery to the dregs that they might be happy, to go naked that they might wear silks and jewels, pay taxes that they might be spared from paying them, be familiar all their lives with the degrading language and postures of adulation that they might walk in pride and think themselves the gods of this world.
—Samuel Clemens,
A Connecticut Yankee in King Arthur's Court

(4) But what can be done to mitigate the fears, to disperse the hatred, violence, and irrationality gathered around school

37

integration, to take the initiative out of the hands of racial demagogues, to release respect for the law?

—Martin Luther King, Jr., *Stride toward Freedom*

adv. - mod able
adv. - forced
adv. - strolling
adv. - leave

(5) These mothers instead of being able to work for their honest livelihood, are forced to employ all their time in strolling to beg sustenance for their helpless infants, who, as they grow up, either turn thieves for want of work, or leave their dear Native Country to fight for the Pretender in Spain or sell themselves to the Barbadoes.

—Jonathan Swift, "A Modest Proposal"

adv. - necessary
(PA)
adv. - able
adv. - necess
adv. - ready
adv. - allow

(6) But it is necessary to be able to disguise this character well, and to be a great feigner and dissembler; and men are so simple and so ready to obey present necessities, that one who deceives will always find those who allow themselves to be deceived.

subj. Inf Clause

passive infinitive

—Niccoló Machiavelli, *The Prince*

Exercise in composition

(EXTRA)

The models above indicate how effectively writers can employ the infinitive. The example below shows how one student writer used the infinitive to help create a vivid scene:

X - prep.

note use of participle & gerund

To stride blandly past the scarlet-clad bellboy's outstretched palm, to lope slowly down the street, his beady eyes sweeping restlessly from edge to edge of the sidewalk, to execute a sloppy military turn at the first corner, to clatter down a red-brick alley, watching sooty shadows in his British black cashmere suit, to astound idlers lounging in tavern doorways by stooping, extending his hand, and dredging up a long-tarnished, long-forgotten dime and about-facing with a gusty, contented sigh—the epitome of secret games the world's most extravagant millionaire liked to play.

—*A student's writing*

assignment

Keeping these excellent examples in mind, write a paragraph using the infinitive construction. — *1 of each type*

Concentrate on one brief incident for which the following information represents the nucleus, describe the scene and make it come to life:

38

Cumulative exercise — economy drill (eg DRIVING — verb, part. (ger.) clause, phrase, etc.

A door opens. A figure stumbles into the dim light. His face is bloody. His arm hangs at his side. His clothes are dirty. He falls to the floor. The lights blink and go out. Darkness.

supplement from Warriner's?

Lesson six — *coordinate constructions*

One of the most fundamental principles of usage, |*parallelism*| unites coordinate elements (words, phrases, clauses, or sentences in the same grammatical form) to indicate that these elements have similar functions or that certain ideas have equal importance.

[*SAME STRUCTURAL PLACE IN DIAGRAM*]

WORDS

The fighting was violent for a few moments, then the pair walked on, *boxing, jostling, parrying.*   *participles*
—Marjorie Kinnan Rawlings, *The Yearling*

PHRASES   *OP - "for" (prep. phrases)* *adv.*

Studies serve *for delight, for ornament, and for ability.*
—Francis Bacon, "Of Studies"

CLAUSES   *prep. phrase followed by adv. clause*

... he submits [to pain,] *because it is inevitable,* [to bereavement,] *because it is irreparable,* and [to death,] *because it is his destiny.*   *adv. clause "because it is - PA"*
—John Newman, "The Gentleman"

SENTENCES   *noun clause - DO   Adv. clause LV (easier) comp.*

It " =
loyalty

It is PN
not

It is easier to say what loyalty is not than what it is. *It is not conformity. It is not passive acquiescence in the status quo. It is not preference for everything American over everything foreign. It is not an ostrich-like ignorance of other countries and other institutions. It is not the indulgence in ceremony—a flag salute, an oath of allegiance, a fervid verbal declaration. It is not a particular creed, a particular version of history, a particular body of economic practices, a particular philosophy.*   *indep. clauses   OP   PN series (Compound)*
—Henry Steele Commager, "Who Is Loyal to America?"

Such balancing provides a method of closely relating a number of ideas and details, and, when those ideas and details become

39

complicated, provides a method of keeping their relationship clear. Skillful use of these constructions may eliminate unnecessary clauses and produce clearer, more concise writing.

How would one achieve clarity and conciseness in the paragraphs below?

> Mrs. Davis went to summer school for three reasons. The first reason was that she had a desire to know more about American history. An increase in salary because of the additional educational experience was her second reason. Also, she was interested in gathering material for a new course in Social Studies.

division

> They sought peace; they got war. They sought fraternity; they divided brother from brother. They sought social justice; they achieved more poverty, more misery, more distress.
> —William F. Russell, "How to Beat Communism"

The example above also illustrates how the repetition of key words or phrases reinforces the coordinate construction. Writers can repeat the introductory word of each parallel construction merely to signal the beginning of an element of parallelism, or, for greater effect, to create an almost hypnotic emphasis. However, when the individual elements become obvious, a writer may only need to use the introductory word before the first element, as in this example:

> My brother need not be idealized, or enlarged in death beyond what he was in life, to be remembered simply as a good and decent man, who saw wrong and tried to right it, saw suffering and tried to heal it, saw war and tried to stop it.
> —Edward M. Kennedy, Eulogy for Robert F. Kennedy

To avoid parallelism when elements contain logical coordination, or to employ parallelism when elements contain none, results in *faulty parallelism*.

AVOIDING PARALLELISM *use 2 gerunds or 2 infinitives*

Her job was washing the dishes and to sweep the floor.
gerund   *infinitive*

FAULTY PARALLELISM *need 2nd clause*

Tom is tall, handsome, and captain of the team.
adj   *adj.*   *noun*

What difficulties do these two sentences have? How would one eliminate the problems?

Exercise in analysis

The fifteen models below contain coordinate constructions. In each we can now point out the examples of parallelism:

(1) Eat not to dullness; drink not to elevation.

— Benjamin Franklin, *Autobiography*

(2) Every sweet has its sour; every evil its good.

— Ralph Waldo Emerson, "Compensation"

(3) There is the careless self taking anything that comes along, excellent and vulgar, fine and cheap.

— Harry Emerson Fosdick, *The Hope of the World*

(4) Not in innocence, and not in Asia, was mankind born.

— Robert Ardrey, *African Genesis*

(5) I shall say no more about the laughter and the excitement, the horror and cruelty of the circus.

— Mika Waltari, *The Etruscan*

(6) Everything of the best was got out for her: the best cups, the best spoons, the best tablecloth, the best coffee-jug.

— D. H. Lawrence, *Sons and Lovers*

(7) These, then, as we said at the beginning, are the three differences which distinguish artistic imitation—the medium, the objects, and the manner.

— Aristotle, *Poetics*

(8) I have learned silence from the talkative, toleration from the intolerant, and kindness from the unkind; yet, strange, I am ungrateful to those teachers.

— Kahlil Gibran, *Sand and Foam*

(9) The war was over, peace had been declared, but the Yankees could still rob her, they could still starve her, they could still drive her from her house.

— Margaret Mitchell, *Gone with the Wind*

(10) He allowed himself to talk of his adolescence, his village, his first studies, his first religious experiences, and his

41

first step in real life—taking care only to situate all these memories not in his own but in the Marsi diocese.

—Ignazio Silone, *Bread and Wine*

(11) If he gives himself up to intellectual adventure, if he tries to do his own thinking, if he attempts to reach conclusions for himself, if he announces and stands by his convictions, he may rest assured his friends will begin by looking at him askance, and probably end by abandoning him altogether.

—Howard Mumford Jones, "The Attractions of Stupidity"

(12) He liked everything about his convoy: he liked its air of purpose as it cracked on speed after the cautious passage down-channel: he liked individual ships—particularly the tough and shapely tankers: he liked the men on board who waved cheerfully to *Compass Rose* as she passed down the line towards the tail of the convoy.

—Nicholas Monsarrat, *The Cruel Sea*

(13) But her parents had taught her the beauties of Africa, its strength, its song, its mighty rivers, its early smelting of iron, its building of the pyramids, and its ancient and important civilizations.

—Langston Hughes, "One Friday Morning"

(14) No matter who came or how large the dinner, Lutie Brewton was the tireless pure flame burning in the center of it, her face flatteringly raised to listen, her talk a highly seasoned language of its own, her headlong treble laughter leading into general bursts of merriment, and her ringed fingers skimming over the white keys of the piano, with the soft light from the tall marble, brass, and china lamp golden on her dark hair.

—Conrad Richter, *The Sea of Grass*

(15) A quick gust of wind brought the rain down with sudden vehemence, and Paul was startled to find that he was still outside in the slush of the gravel driveway; that his boots were letting in the water and his scanty overcoat was clinging wet behind him; that the lights in front of the concert hall were out, and that the rain was driving in sheets between him and the orange glow of the windows above him.

—Willa Cather, "Paul's Case"

42

Parallelism has an inherent quality that can bring dignity to an occasion and impressiveness to the words. This frequently results in a quotability, a certain something that makes a phrase easy to remember, a certain something that makes a phrase or a sentence impressive.

Formal occasions frequently produce memorable words; Lincoln's Gettysburg Address and Kennedy's Inaugural Address both effectively illustrate the advantages of being able to construct sentences with skill and force. The use of parallelism marks both these speeches. *find copies*

The occasion does not, of course, have to be formal to permit the use of coordinate structure. But this does not mean to suggest its indiscriminate use either. Excessive use or inappropriate placement can hamper writing, in which timing must have its place. Words, phrases, clauses, and sentences, whether in parallel construction or not, have to be arranged with careful attention to sound and meaning if a writer wishes to use these tools to their fullest.

Exercise in rewriting

Keeping in mind what has been said and what has been revealed through the above models, improve each of the following by correcting the faulty parallelism or by adding a parallel structure:

(1) Judy likes to cook and do sewing.

(2) He was always well mannered, well dressed, and an excellent scholar.

(3) After developing a new slogan, the advertising agency tests its appeal and then its conclusions are drawn.

(4) She was the young woman with the highest scores on the tests and who had the best academic record in the class.

(5) The purpose of the gathering was threefold: bringing together people with like political interests, to select a representative for the convention, and they also began making campaign plans for the fall.

(6) Aquinas's argument for the existence of God includes five proofs, which are motion, first cause, the argument of

necessity, gradation, and finally the concluding argument which is the governing of things.

(7) When I entered his den, I saw a large desk with a typewriter and paper on it, posters covering the wall; then I saw several bookcases jammed with hardbacks and paperbacks and in a corner papers and notebooks covered a wobbly table.

(8) Sports fans show their disapproval in many ways. They boo. Some shout comments at the referees and players. They make excessive amounts of noise to disturb the players. Some throw objects, like bottles, seat cushions, or paper cups. Sometimes their anger becomes violent and they brawl among themselves, with the police, or with the players.

Exercise in composition

In the exercise above we worked with parallelism in a rather limited way, correcting the faults of others. Now, to extend that experience, we will experiment with writing at paragraph length, using coordinate constructions as the basic pattern or framework. The topic for your paragraph is:

I remember . . .

These two words may function as an opening or a closing, or may be repeated to signal the items remembered. The paragraph —a single sentence or a series of parallel sentences—may follow the "I remember" with the thing or things remembered or with some mark of punctuation, such as three dots, a dash, a colon. Let the memories flow, but take care to distinguish one element from another and to call attention to each element through balanced construction.

Lesson seven — the absolute (SKIP?)

The *absolute* or *nominative absolute*—one of the most common syntactic structures and a frequently used free modifier—*designates a phrase related to the thought of a sentence, but not related grammatically to any word in that sentence*)(that is to say, the absolute does not modify anything). We can, as an example, write the following sentence:

44

The snow *having stopped,* we went home. *(part. phr.)*

Here, the absolute phrase modifies no single word in the independent clause of the sentence, but obviously the thought within the absolute relates to the thought within the independent clause.

Technically, absolutes avoid classification as a clause because they do not contain a subject and a verb; however, they probably stem from the adverb clause. One might begin the following sentence with an adverb clause:

Since the day was windy, I wore an overcoat.

Converting the dependent clause into a nominative absolute results in this sentence:

The day *being windy,* I wore an overcoat. *(part. phr.)*

Such constructions usually consist of a noun or a pronoun and a participle (stated or understood), either with or without modifiers.

ABSOLUTE WITH PARTICIPLE STATED

The job *being finished,* we left. *(part. phr.)*

ABSOLUTE WITH PARTICIPLE UNDERSTOOD

The film *over,* the students went home.

Any group of directly related words help form the *absolute phrase,* which we generally set off from the rest of the sentence by commas.

Absolutes offer the writer an effective means of adding details in a minimum number of words.

Exercise in analysis

The eight models below, including the Evan Hunter example in the composition exercise, illustrate the wide use of the nominative absolute. Determine the following for each of them:

a. the absolute or absolutes in each model
b. how each absolute relates to the sentence. *(non-grammatical)*

(1) Roy circled the bases like a Mississippi steamboat, lights lit, flags fluttering, whistle banging, coming round the bend.
—Bernard Malamud, *The Natural*

(2) All through the dark street he strained against the ropes, his body naked and streaming with sweating, and his bare feet slipping on the cobbles, slimy and wet as they were with the dampness of the night.

—Pearl S. Buck, *The Good Earth*

(3) The two transports had sneaked up from the south in the first graying flush of dawn, their cumbersome mass cutting smoothly through the water whose still greater mass bore them silently, themselves as grey as the dawn which camouflaged them.

—James Jones, *The Thin Red Line*

(4) It is against the background of Ripton, then, that I picture Frost hearing thrush music, as it is there that I recall him in many other postures; a stocky figure but alert in motion, wearing an old suit and scuffed shoes, freshly laundered soft shirt open at his throat, his white hair tousled in the wind, his seafarer's blue eyes twinkling.

—George Frisbie Whicher, "Out for Stars:
A Meditation on Robert Frost"

(5) We number our highways nowadays, our speed being so great we can remember little of their quality or character and are lucky to remember their number.

—E. B. White, "Walden"

(6) The motorcyclists stopped their machines, leaned them up against the entrance columns, and then took up positions beside the doorways, their faces expressionless under their black leather helmets, their hands on the revolvers in their belts.

—Alberto Moravia, *Two Women*

(7) An airshaft: cabbage and chitterlings cooking; liver and onions sizzling, sputtering; three player-pianos out-plunking each other; a man and a woman calling each other vile things; a sick, neglected baby wailing; a phonograph broadcasting blues; dishes clacking; a girl crying heartbrokenly; waste noises, waste odors of a score of families, seeking issue through a common channel; pollution from bottom to top— sewer of sounds and smells.

—Rudolph Fisher, "The City of Refuge"

Exercise in composition

The following paragraph has been selected not only because it uses the absolute structure but also because it vividly describes a specific scene. Because he has selected his words with extreme care, Evan Hunter, the author, makes it possible for the reader to visualize his storm:

> It started in the early hours of the morning, while the city slept. The snowflakes filtered down from a cast-iron sky, lazily at first, large wet flakes that melted the instant they touched the pavement. The darkened, empty streets took on a glistening in the wan light of the street lamps. And then the snow began in earnest. The big, sloppy, wet flakes fled before an onslaught of smaller, sharper white. The wind swept the snow over the pavements and gutters, and the snow clung and whirled and clung again. The street lamps stood like sentries at attention, their yellow-capped heads erect, the snow lashing at them, swirling about them. The snow covered. Slowly, patiently, it devoured black patches of asphalt, smothered the gray concrete, lodged in the brown earth of open lots, caked on the chipped paint of window sills, heaped against the curbs and bases of the lamp posts, dropped a clinging downy-wet blanket on the metal-bottle tops of the parked automobiles.
>
> —Evan Hunter, *The Blackboard Jungle*

Now, with the use of the nominative absolute, with the use of very specific sentences, and with the use of carefully chosen words, construct a paragraph with the following material as its germ or nucleus.

Darkness. Four men carrying and then setting down a box. A crowd waiting. Anticipation.

Lesson eight — subordination (the dependent clauses)

A writer's technique must reveal his ability to decide between what has importance to his story and what does not, for it stands to reason that the more significant thoughts need to be emphasized, while the less significant need to be subordinated. In fact, the ability to subordinate the importance of some ideas illustrates, in part, the maturity of a writer.

A dependent or subordinate clause consists of a group of words that contains a subject and predicate and which, not usually making sense when standing alone, depends upon the sentence for its meaning. Operating like any single part of speech, they function as adjectives, adverbs, or nouns.

ADJECTIVE CLAUSE

He returned to the school *where he first taught.*

ADVERB CLAUSE

If he wins today, he will be crowned the new champion.

NOUN CLAUSE

She said *she had done all the work.*

Two important uses of subordinate clauses—to show relationships and to combine thoughts—indicate their value to the writer. Normal positioning, even of connected ideas, does not always accurately suggest their relationship. For example, one could write this sentence:

Students celebrate; the school year is over.

But subordination allows a writer to become more precise:

Students celebrate *when the school year is over.*

Effective combinations of sentences such as this can eliminate the short, choppy statements that so often dominate the style of the inexperienced writer.

Exercise in analysis

Professional writers rely heavily upon dependent clauses, as the eleven models below reveal. For each example we should be able to determine the following:

a. each dependent clause
b. what type each clause is—adjective, adverb, noun
c. what each clause modifies or how each functions

(1) "The truth is that the Turks hold trumps in this particular game, that we have to mind our p's and q's and keep well within the limits of the possible."

—Franz Werfel, *The Forty Days of Musa Dagh*

(2) He had seen her when she was tired, upset and weak, when the shadows came over her eyes, when the fit of her skirt was wrong and she had cold hands, cold lips parted on her teeth, when she was lying on her sofa, a woman of short frame, very full, but after all, a tired, short woman whose breath had the ashen flavor of fatigue.

—Saul Bellow, *Herzog*

(3) The death of the great white oak which gave my grandfather's Indiana homestead its name and which played such an important part in our daily lives was so gentle a transition that we never knew just when it ceased to be a living organism.

—Edwin Way Teale, "The Death of a Tree"

(4) When I had been there a little longer, and had seen this phase of crystal clearness followed by long stretches of sunless cold; when the storms of February had pitched their white tents about the devoted village and wild cavalry of March winds had charged down to their support; I began to understand why Starkfield emerged from its six months' siege like a starved garrison capitulating without quarter.

—Edith Wharton, *Ethan Frome*

(5) If it were not for the artificial fires of merriment, the rush of profit-seeking trade, and pleasure-selling amusements; if the various merchants failed to make the customary display within and without their establishments; if our streets were not strung with signs of gorgeous hues and thronged with hurrying purchasers, we would quickly discover how firmly the chill hand of winter lays upon the heart; how dispiriting are the days during which the sun withholds a portion of our allowance of light and warmth.

—Theodore Dreiser, *Sister Carrie*

(6) Each morning he walked to the workshop by a circuitous route which enabled him to tap all his sources; by the time he reached Ghirlandaio's he had a shopping basketful of

the night's news: who had been cuckolded, who was going to be commissioned for what art project, who was about to be put in stocks with his back against the Signoria wall.

—Irving Stone, *The Agony and the Ecstasy*

(7) But it leaves us with a task: because we cannot make war, because we cannot achieve peace, we must find some other way of meeting the great issues which confront us.

—Walter Lippmann, "The Nuclear Age"

(8) If Fischoff fumbled, if he had cried out from a desire to speak and not with a message, if he fumbled now, this man unused to speech, or spoke uncertainly, there would be chaos.

—Morton Thompson, *The Cry and the Covenant*

(9) He could never understand why he received this attention, why he was singled out as something special.

—Thomas Lee Bucky with Joseph P. Blank, "Einstein: An Intimate Memoir"

(10) They were eyes that masked the soul with a thousand guises, and that sometimes opened, at rare moments, and allowed it to rush up as though it were about to fare forth nakedly into the world on some wonderful adventure,—eyes that could brood with the hopeless sombreness of leaden skies; that could snap and crackle points of fire like those which sparkle from a whirling sword; that could grow chill as an arctic landscape, and yet again, that could warm and soften and be all a-dance with love-lights, intense and masculine, luring and compelling, which at the same time fascinate and dominate women till they surrender in a gladness of joy and of relief and sacrifice.

—Jack London, *The Sea Wolf*

(11) The military party denies neither the bestiality nor the horror, nor the expense; it only says that these things tell but half the story. It only says that war is worth them; that, taking human nature as a whole, its wars are its best protection against its weaker and more cowardly self, and that mankind cannot afford to adopt a peace-economy.

—William James, "The Moral Equivalent of War"

Exercise in composition

DO
NOUN

I notice that my right hand has a slender, wandering, tur-
quoise-blue vein protruding at its base and taking a winding,
spiral route to the flesh of my double-jointed thumb. There
it encounters a mole, dark in earlier years, now resembling a
speck of dirt. The vein, branching, continues down the
middle of my palm while numerous jagged creases terminate
horizontally and vertically over it. On the fourth finger, just
above a half-peeled, popped blister, a narrow gold band that
slips down easily reveals an indentation identical to the
width of the band.

ADV
Continue

ADJ
band

—*A student's writing*

Using three subordinate clauses, the above paragraph illustrates
the ability to set down information without including the author's
own comments. This writer objectively describes his hand, simply
stating those qualities that describe its personality.

Write a paragraph that uses dependent clauses, that describes
a scene, and that reports the things witnessed, but not the things
felt. The following pieces of information will serve as a nucleus
for your paragraph:

On a lonely country road, the narrator sees the body of an old
woman—face down, with spots of blood about her. A bloody
hat lies nearby, a single shoe in the ditch. On a bank at the
other side of the road an even older woman sits next to a
damaged car; she stares into space.

3

Rhetoric
of productive sentences

Introduction

In the two previous chapters, and more especially in the Chapter Two review of syntactic structures, we used examples of writing from professionals who have a complete understanding of their craft. How many times have we read something of a quality similar to these models and said to ourselves, "I wish I could say it that well" or "I wonder how he does it"? This question, and questions like it, may have at best only partial answers. By analyzing, understanding the writing process, by knowing the criteria for mature style and the various methods of word arrangement, we will move closer to an answer.

The language devices already presented in this book and the material yet to come help explain the manner in which a writer presents facts and ideas effectively. They say, in short, that possible ways exist to express facts and ideas and that the writer must be the judge of how best to achieve clearness, persuasiveness, and attractiveness. This, then, basically suggests the concept of *rhetoric*, which we may define as *the presentation of both facts and ideas in clear language, in convincing language, and in attractive language.*

This rhetoric must be a *productive rhetoric that causes the writer to generate or produce clear, convincing, and attractive writing.* This definition comes from Professor Francis Christensen of the University of Southern California, who called it "generative rhetoric," which simply means a "productive rhetoric" or rhetoric that generates ideas.

To understand this generative rhetoric, we must analyze prose sentences and paragraphs. If the examples that follow accurately illustrate part of the process of writing, then this will give us a new way of looking at writing, a way that has more meaning because it forces us to relate consciously the various parts of a sentence. And by understanding their relationships, we can appreciate their importance to good writing as a whole. Ultimately, then, we will be able to move toward greater maturity in our own writing. To help us move in this direction, toward an understanding of productive rhetoric, let us examine Professor Christensen's four basic principles—*addition, texture, levels of generality,* and *direction of movement.*

The principle of addition

We will begin with two paragraphs purposely cut down, basically leaving just the independent clauses:

> I got to my feet a little slowly and began to trot toward Curry, but I saw that there would be no reason for haste. He had been hit again, and was dead now. He lay on his back. His hands and face were dark.
>
> I could not see the wound; there was no spout of blood, and a wrinkled sheet of blood was settling. The wounds of the second barrage I could scarcely miss.

Counting the words in each of the sentences in the above, cut-down paragraphs gives these statistics:

SENTENCE	NUMBER OF WORDS
1	25
2	9
3	5
4	6
5	20
6	10

What is the average number of words in each of the six sentences above? According to the chart in Chapter One, what level of writing might this represent? Do these paragraphs show an ability to present the long sentence effectively?

The writer could have written the above paragraphs as they have been presented here; he did not. Below, the author's material has been restored to its original form, with the previously omitted words set in italics:

> I got to my feet a little slowly, *with belly and chest darkly washed by a fine, silt-like mud,* and began to trot toward Curry, but *even before I reached him* I saw there would be no reason for haste. He had been hit again, and was dead now. He lay on his back, *arms outspread against the rainy Holland earth.* His hands and face were dark, *with the weathering that comes to the devoted infantryman.*
>
> I could not see the wound *that had first caught him;* there was no spout of blood *to define it now,* and a wrinkled sheet of blood was settling *all along his throat and collarbone and down his right shoulder.* The wounds of the second barrage I could scarcely miss, *for they were a great slash across his right thigh and a rip all across his belly, out of which now tumbled bowels and intestines.*
>
> —Edward Loomis, "Wounds"

What average number of words do these six sentences now have? What level of writing does this now represent? Does Loomis show the ability to write and control the long sentence?

The difference between the cut-down paragraphs and the original paragraphs involves more than length of sentence and average number of words per sentence; it involves a concept of mature writing.

The first set of two paragraphs had been cut down intentionally not only to illustrate the difference in styles, but also, and probably more importantly, to demonstrate the manner in which writers write. Writing, in simple terms, appears to be a process of putting down a base clause, a main clause, or main idea, and expanding it through the addition of further important pieces of information, both before and after the main, or base, clause. For example, in the Loomis paragraphs at least four of the italicized word groupings (in each case, a type of free modifier) have been added and set off with commas. Loomis might have written:

The wounds of the second barrage I could scarcely miss.

One could accept this word grouping as a legitimate English sentence. But, after this base clause, Loomis adds a free modifier, in this case a long adverb clause, set off by a comma. This process of addition creates a forceful sentence:

The wounds of the second barrage I could scarcely miss, *for they were a great slash across his right thigh and a rip all across his belly, out of which now tumbled bowels and intestines.*

On the other hand, Loomis might have written:

I saw there would be no reason for haste.

Instead, he precedes his base clause with an additional and necessary adverb clause:

. . . *even before I reached him* I saw there would be no reason for haste.

Turning to another writer, B. J. Chute, the following passes as a grammatically acceptable base clause:

She stood still and didn't feel anything at all.

But Chute expands the thought and improves the sentence with the addition of a free modifier structure, an introductory adverb clause:

When she heard Mrs. Mitchell's key in the lock, she stood still and didn't feel anything at all.

—B. J. Chute, "The Blue Cup"

So, by cutting down the original Loomis paragraphs and by analyzing the construction of two sentences from Loomis's short story and another sentence from Chute's short story, we see how a writer adds to his main ideas and main clauses to produce a gloss on his finished product. As a final example, we have a clause barely acceptable as a message from the writer:

Until then I'm a long-distance runner.

Alone, it tells us nothing, really. But, when the author adds a type of free modifier, a participial clause, it acts as a postscript, or footnote, making the base clause seem a precise expression of feeling:

Until then I'm a long-distance runner, *crossing country all on my own no matter how bad it feels.*
      —Alan Sillitoe,
         "The Loneliness of the Long-Distance Runner"

The models above, in which the writers make good use of the base clause and the principle of addition, clearly demonstrate one means of producing clear, convincing, and attractive writing.

The principle of texture

Actually, the principle of texture has already been demonstrated in the Loomis paragraphs. Employing the principle of addition, by using free modifiers, Loomis changed the texture of his writing. And his style has a rich, mature quality, just as a brocade has a rich, full texture. And just as burlap has a simple, bare texture, so the cut-down paragraphs on page 53 have a plain, bare style.

Grammatically and technically, the cut-down paragraphs have nothing wrong with them. The sentences follow the basic patterns of all sentences—the shorter pattern includes simply the subject, verb, and modifiers, at most only four or five words, one of them being a verb; the longer pattern includes the subject, verb, indirect object, and direct object, plus modifiers, at least seven or eight words, one of them being a verb.

It would appear, then, that the average English prose sentence contains one verb, or verbal, for every five to eight words. Analysis by Bernard R. Tanner reveals that good modern prose writers almost invariably use a high proportion of verbs in relation to their total number of words. He calls this *verb density.* Sentences with one verb or verbal for every five to eight words (1:5 to 1:8) have *high verb density;* sentences with one verb or verbal for every nine words or more (1:9) have *low verb density.*

Verb density is a key to the improvement of texture in writing and, if properly used, can prevent writing from bogging down and becoming muddy in meaning. But of course, no exact formula will produce good writing. If we examine both the cut-down paragraphs and the original Loomis paragraphs used on page 54, we discover that both have verb densities well within the "acceptable" ratio—the cut-down version has

14 verbs and verbals in 75 words or a ratio of about 1:5; the uncut version has 24 verbs and verbals and 152 words or a ratio of about 1:6. But certainly the rich, mature style and texture of the Loomis original is preferable to the bare, sixth-grade level and style of the cut-down version. This should indicate, then, that the principle of texture depends on another quality even more than verb density. This basic, though less visible, quality might best be termed "variety"; but defining it becomes as difficult as defining the abstract idea of texture itself. Variety probably comes closest to being what we understand as a writer's personal style, his own way of using words, and, ultimately, what makes his writing of great or of little consequence.

What can be done to improve the texture of the following sentence? And, more especially, what can be done to improve both the verb density and the maturity of style?

> A golfer, after four long hours in a row in the sun on the course, received a challenge for a nine-hole match from his friend and accepted it wearily and regretfully.

Although the principle of texture will be seen again and again in the examples to be used, the model below will serve to illustrate how one writer makes full and competent use of verbal structures in his writing. Here is his sentence base:

> They all paused.

Adding to this several free modifiers (an adverb before the base and a participial phrase and a nominative absolute after the base), he is able to produce a dense, richly textured sentence:

> *Abruptly,* they all paused, *holding their clothes in their hands, their attention caught by a light tapping in the thinly plastered walls of the room.*
>
> —Richard Wright, *Native Son*

The principle of levels of generality

To write prose with a dense texture requires a close examination of precisely that kind of writing. We can accomplish this by studying the principle of levels of generality within sentences. Levels of generality, or modifying structures, simply refer to those groupings of words that, when added to the main clause of a sentence, make the base clause progressively more concrete and more specific, in a cumulative rather than in an individual way. Quite often writers use punctuation to indicate additional modifying structures or levels. These levels include the free modifiers and syntactic structures reviewed in Chapter Two—the appositive, the verbals, the absolute, and the clauses.

If a writer adds only one grouping of words, it must refer to the main clause or sentence base (presuming, of course, the addition does not represent another independent clause). If it does not refer to the base and if it does not amount to another independent clause, then it does not belong to the sentence. To illustrate, we will diagram a sentence, using "1" to indicate the base clause and "2" to indicate the addition. Both the base and the specific type of free modifier added will be labeled in parentheses.

BASE CLAUSE WITH ONE ADDED ELEMENT

The trail was deep, with round rocks that kept causing the animals to slip.

—Jack Kerouac, "Alone on a Mountain Top"

1 The trail was deep, (base)
   2 with round rocks that kept causing the animals to slip. (expanded prepositional phrase)

A writer may also construct a sentence with two independent clauses and add a free modifier to one of them.

TWO BASE CLAUSES WITH ONE ADDED ELEMENT

You may tell me that this was against nature; but to be human consists precisely in transcending nature—in overcoming the biological limitations that we have inherited from our prehuman ancestors.

—Arnold Toynbee,
"Why I Dislike Western Civilization"

1 You may tell me that this was against nature; (base)
1 but to be human consists precisely in transcending nature— (base)
   2 in overcoming the biological limitations that we have inherited from our prehuman ancestors. (prepositional phrase)

Or, a writer may link several independent clauses together without any dependent additions.

THREE BASE CLAUSES WITH NO ADDED ELEMENTS

His hair was white and thinning, his eyes were alert, his nose was high-bridged with nostrils like a horse's.
—Stephen Becker, *A Covenant with Death*

1 His hair was white and thinning, (base)
1 his eyes were alert, (base)
1 his nose was high-bridged with nostrils like a horse's. (base)

Sometimes a writer will place a structure between the subject and verb of his base clause. In Chapter One we called this *the medial position for free modifiers.*

SPLIT LEVEL ONE WITH ONE ADDED ELEMENT

The house, covered with unpainted weatherboards, sat precariously on the three piles of thin stones.
—Erskine Caldwell, *Tobacco Road*

1 The house, . . . , sat precariously on three piles of thin stones. (base)
    2 covered with unpainted weatherboards (participial phrase)

The principle of direction of movement

The examples used so far have been very simple, a sentence base, with a single modifying structure. Any further additions will, of course, help to indicate the flow or *direction of movement* of the sentence. These further additions to a sentence may either refer to the base clause and coordinate with it (one type of sentence movement), or refer to the addition immediately preceding it and thus be subordinate to it (a second distinct type of movement). The following model, using a series of three noun clauses, illustrates the coordinated construction that produces intra-T-unit coordination in the sentence. Here, all the noun clause additions refer directly to the base, or level one, clause:

The rewards of the struggle are bountiful: the eye is continually delighted and refreshed, the heart is eased by the imposition of simplicity upon it, the intellect admires the imperious rages of the elements and the Yankee refusal to be cowed by them.

—Jean Stafford, "New England Winter"

1 The rewards of the struggle are bountiful: (base)
  2 the eye is continually delighted and refreshed, (noun clause appositive)
  2 the heart is eased by the imposition of simplicity upon it, (noun clause appositive)
  2 the intellect admires the imperious rages of the elements and the Yankee refusal to be cowed by them. (noun clause appositive)

The level two constructions do not depend on other level two constructions for communication with the level one or base, but communicate directly with level one. The following diagram graphically illustrates this coordinated movement:

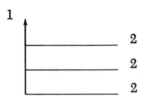

A second example demonstrates subordinated construction, in which the levels move away from the sentence base. This subordination becomes clearer when we diagram the sentence, using "1" to indicate the base clause, "2" to indicate the grouping of words referring to level one, and "3" to indicate the grouping of words referring to level two:

At first glance we are alien to this idea, because man is particularly a creature who has turned the tables on his environment so that he is now engrossed in shaping it, rather than being shaped by it.

—Loren C. Eiseley,
    "Man and the Porpoise: Two Solitary Destinies"

1 At first glance we are alien to this idea, (base)
  2 because man is particularly a creature who has turned

the tables on his environment so that he is now engrossed in shaping it,   (adverb clause)
3 rather than being shaped by it.   (adverbial phrase)

In this example, level three refers to the level two and level two
refers to level one. Thus, level three communicates with level
one only through level two. Again, we can graphically illustrate
this movement:

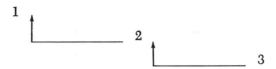

Writers frequently use this subordinated movement. In the model
below, you will notice that the author follows his base clause
with a dash.

BASE CLAUSE WITH TWO SUBORDINATED ELEMENTS

I noticed for the first time how well it matched her voice—a
beautiful hand, firm and intelligent and good-natured.
                              —Hermann Hesse, *Steppenwolf*

1 I noticed for the first time how well it matched her voice—
   (base)
  2 a beautiful hand,   (appositive)
    3 firm and intelligent and good-natured.   (adjective
      phrase)

A writer need not stop after adding two subordinated elements. He may continue adding levels as long as he does not
destroy the effectiveness and the flow of his sentence.

BASE CLAUSE WITH THREE SUBORDINATED ELEMENTS

A sudden emptiness seemed to flow now from the windows
and the great doors, endowing with complete isolation the
figure of the host, who stood on the porch, his hand up in a
formal gesture of farewell.
                              —F. Scott Fitzgerald, *The Great Gatsby*

1 A sudden emptiness seemed to flow now from the windows
   and the great doors,   (base)

2 endowing with complete isolation the figure of the host, (participial phrase)
   3 who stood on the porch, (adjective clause)
     4 his hand up in a formal gesture of farewell. (absolute)

Similarly, a writer need not stop after adding three coordinated levels. The model below achieves strong intra-T-unit coordination with its four level two structures. Although, in this clause, the writer does not use any punctuation after the fourth level two, what follows clearly represents a second base clause.

ONE BASE CLAUSE WITH FOUR COORDINATED LEVELS
AND A SECOND BASE CLAUSE

One entire row of tables and stalls deals in nothing but blazing bananas, golden fingers clutched in clumps and clusters, yellow masses piled high, great green claws hanging down, and golden crowns swirling like blazing haloes as they hang on strings and the air is alive with the gold of bananas and the smell of their heady ferment.

           —Agnes Newton Keith, *Bare Feet in the Palace*

1 One entire row of tables and stalls deals in nothing but blazing bananas, (base)
  2 golden fingers clutched in clumps and clusters, (appositive)
  2 yellow masses piled high, (appositive)
  2 great green claws hanging down, and (appositive)
  2 golden crowns swirling like blazing haloes as they hang on strings and (appositive)
1 the air is alive with the gold of bananas and the smell of their heady ferment. (base)

And, of course, free modifiers can precede the base clause as well as follow it.

ONE ADDED ELEMENT PRECEDING THE BASE CLAUSE
WITH TWO SUBORDINATED ELEMENTS FOLLOWING THE BASE

Anyhow, it was too hot for a fire, although a fire might have been a heavy help against the mosquitoes, which were now beginning a concerted dive on my carcass.

           —Robert Ruark, "Good-bye, Cruel World"

2 Anyhow, (adverb)
1 it was too hot for a fire, (base)
   2 although a fire might have been a heavy help against
   the mosquitoes, (adverb clause)
      3 which were now beginning a concerted dive on my
      carcass. (adjective clause)

Far from avoiding the smile, as Camden's habit was, the
storekeeper returned it with a brotherly wink for good
measure.

—Wilbur Daniel Steele, "Blue Murder"

   2 Far from avoiding the smile, (adjective phrase)
      3 as Camden's habit was, (adverb clause)
1 the storekeeper returned it with a brotherly wink for good
measure. (base)

Exercises in analysis

The excellent models in these exercises, containing progressively more complex sentences, illustrate how addition, texture,
levels, and direction blend together, to present material effectively. Using the sentences on the preceding pages as guides,
diagram the sentences in the following three exercises and indicate both the levels of each element and the function or direction
of each level.

EXERCISE ONE

(1) All he let her see was his usual spell of coughing before
retiring, his usual half-hearted caress and opaque manner
of approach, his usual resignation, his usual sleeping posture,
curled up like a dormant chrysalis.

—Yukio Mishima, *After the Banquet*

(2) She was genial and gay and made them all laugh about
her leave, which she had taken because she felt she deserved
it, not because the Maharani said she might go.

—E. M. Forster, *A Passage to India*

(3) Ed Pauley, the officer-of-the-deck, was sitting on a bitt
reading an Ellery Queen story, and Farnsworth, the mes-

senger, was poring over a comic book when Farnsworth glanced over the side and saw this most remarkable thing.

—Thomas Heggen, *Mister Roberts*

(4) There were a lot of things to do, such as making my leather boots more waterproof by rubbing lard on them, putting my stamp collection in order, sharpening a deer's-foot knife I had recently acquired, winding tape on my new hockey stick, or reading one of the half-dozen books I had bought with my last birthday money.

—Ben Hecht, "Snowfall in Childhood"

(5) With George Willard, son of Tom Willard, the proprietor of the new Willard House, he had formed something like a friendship.

—Sherwood Anderson, *Winesburg, Ohio*

(6) His features were good—a straight nose, firm mouth, broad forehead, from which his long, dark hair was combed straight back, falling behind his ears to the collar of his well-fitting frock coat.

—Ambrose Bierce, "An Occurrence at Owl Creek Bridge"

(7) Searched for, plenty of familiarities are there: the Pastime Theater, identical with the one that sits across Main Street from the firehouse in my mind; the lumber yard where we used to get cloth caps advertising DeLaval Cream Separators; two or three hardware stores (a prairie wheat town specializes in hardware stores), though each one now has a lot full of farm machinery next to it; the hotel, just as it was rebuilt after the fire; the bank, now remodeled into the post office; the Presbyterian church, now United, and the Leader office, and the square brick prison of the school, now with three smaller prisons added to it.

—Wallace Stegner, *Wolf Willow*

(8) When a few minutes later the warden turned the light off from outside, and looked through the spy-hole into his cell, Rubashov, ex-Commissar of the People, slept, his back turned to the wall, with his head on his outstretched left arm, which stuck stiffly out of the bed; only the hand on the end of it hung loosely and twitched in his sleep.

—Arthur Koestler, *Darkness at Noon*

(1)   They were the family from the nearest farm, a mother, father and two children, dressed in discarded uniforms and brandishing rakes.

—James Michener, *The Bridges at Toko-Ri*

(2)   She would be rich and lovely ... with a velvet dress and a long sweeping plume ... under the moon ... and the night wind ... that felt of your body with its long, slender fingers ... that tapered at the ends.

—Bess Streeter Aldrich, *A Lantern in Her Hand*

(3)   As he stared mournfully out the window at the great raw land so sparsely tilled by the futile and occasional little farms, which seemed to have made only little grubbing patches in the wilderness, his heart went cold and leaden in him.

—Thomas Wolfe, *Look Homeward, Angel*

(4)   Observant parents were there, planning for the future bliss of their nearest and dearest;—mothers and fathers of handsome lads, lithe and elegant as young pines, and fresh from the polish of foreign university training; mothers and fathers of splendid girls whose simplest attitudes were witcheries.

—Lafcadio Hearn, "The Storm"

(5)   He turned over and floated, spouting the water, pretending he was the most powerful whale in the seas and oceans, floating along, minding its business, because all the sharks were leery of attacking it.

—James T. Farrell, *Young Lonigan*

(6)   As Patsy saw his mother growing worse, saw her gasping for breath, heard the rattling as she drew in the little air that kept going her clogged lungs, felt the heat of her burning hands, and saw the pitiful appeal in her poor eyes, he became convinced that the city doctor was not helping her.

—Paul Lawrence Dunbar, "The Finish of Patsy Barnes"

(7)   The mothers kept "well out of the way," as Mrs. Hack enthusiastically put it; kept, in fact, to their own comfort-

able adult preserve—the veranda and the card room—and their own adult timetable—an early, quiet breakfast before the young people, who had been out till all hours, came in to make the dining room restless; a walk or a chat, followed by a quick bathe and a quick retreat from the hot beach back to the cool of the hotel; a long sleep in the afternoon; bridge in the evening.

—Nadine Gordimer, "A Company of Laughing Faces"

(8)   At the front of the hall, standing before the small stage, was a young German *Obersturmführer*, and beside him a rather fat civilian in a black suit, evidently also German, who from time to time tugged at a watch chain, hanging thick and garish as bunting across his globular vest, and pulled out an enormous watch, the covered face of which he snapped open with a loud click and then snapped shut again, barely looking at the time but reminding the men assembled before him of its passage by the impatient, repeated *click-click   click-click* of the cover.

—John Hersey, *The Wall*

EXERCISE THREE

(1)   When he entered his father's office in Buenos Aires, a large room severe and modern as a laboratory, with photographs of the properties of d'Anconia Copper as sole ornament on its walls—photographs of the greatest mines, ore docks and foundries in the world—he saw, in the place of honor, facing his father's desk, a photograph of the Cleveland foundry with the new sign above its gate.

—Ayn Rand, *Atlas Shrugged*

(2)   They were on their way to see Ivan Ivanovich Voskoboinkov, a teacher and author of popular textbooks, who lived at Duplyanka, the estate of Kologrivov, a silk manufacturer, and a great patron of the arts.

—Boris Pasternak, *Doctor Zhivago*

(3)   The concrete highway was edged with a mat of tangled, broken dry grass, and the grass heads were heavy with cat beards to catch on a dog's coat, and foxtails to tangle in a horse's fetlocks, and clover burrs to fasten in sheep's wool; sleeping life waiting to be spread and dispersed, every

seed armed with an appliance of dispersal, twisting darts and parachutes for the wind, little spears and balls of tiny thorns, all waiting for animals and for the wind, for a man's trouser cuff or the hem of a woman's skirt, all passive but armed with the appliances of activity, still, but each possessed of the anlage of movement.

—John Steinbeck, *The Grapes of Wrath*

(4) It was, like most teutonic architecture of the period, a pompous and finicky affair when it was finished, built up as it was in the middle of the lake, with long straight embankments across the water, upon which the royal coaches could drive up in all their splendor, reflected, head down, in the clear surface, as had been the stag, surrounded by the Queen's hounds.

—Isak Dinesen, "The Poet"

(5) But the tenseness, even with her back turned; it was still in the classroom, emphasized because of the emptiness, magnified, made precise, his mind and her mind, their grief, side by side, conflicting; why?

—William Saroyan, "Laughter"

(6) But, all the same, intolerable pictures broke through— her mother at the sink; her mother ironing; her mother standing between the lace curtains, staring out at the dreary street with a wounded look in her eyes; her mother tying the same lace curtains with yellow ribbons; attempts at lightness, gaiety, which came to nothing; her mother gathering her huge black cat to her, burying her face in its fur while a great shivering sigh—of despair, of boredom—escaped her.

—Elizabeth Taylor, "The First Death in Her Life"

(7) As I drove, faded and yellowed pictures of the school's early days displayed in the library flashed across the screen of my mind, coming fitfully and fragmentarily to life— photographs of men and women in wagons drawn by mule teams and oxen, dressed in black, dusty clothing, people who seemed almost without individuality, a black mob that seemed to be waiting, looking with blank faces, and among them the inevitable collection of white men and women in smiles, clear of features, striking and elegant and confident.

—Ralph Ellison, *Invisible Man*

(8) Gabe was his hostler, a big, ape-like man, stronger than was natural, but weak-minded; not crazy, but childish, like his mind had never grown up.

—Walter Van Tilburg Clark, *The Ox-Bow Incident*

Exercise in composition

So far we have isolated these examples, a single sentence at a time, each taken out of context. We must now look at a complete paragraph to see how the dense texture of one sentence, heavy with free modifiers, enhances the whole.

He sat on the logs, smoking, drying in the sun, the sun warm on his back, the river shallow ahead entering the woods, curving into the woods, shallows, light glittering, big water-smooth rocks, cedars along the bank and white birches, the logs warm in the sun, smooth to sit on, without bark, gray to the touch; slowly the feeling of disappointment left him. It went away slowly, the feeling of disappointment that came sharply after the thrill that made his shoulders ache. It was all right now. His rod lying out on the logs, Nick tied a new hook on the leader, pulling the gut tight until it grimped into itself in a hard knot.

—Ernest Hemingway, "Big Two-Hearted River"

If we diagram the first sentence of Hemingway's paragraph, we discover a very dense and a very complicated structure:

1. He sat on the logs,   (base)
   2 smoking,   (participle)
   2 drying in the sun,   (participial phrase)
      3 the sun warm on his back,   (absolute)
   2 the river shallow ahead entering the woods,   (absolute)
      3 curving into the woods,   (participial phrase)
      3 shallows,   (appositive)
      3 light glittering,   (absolute)
      3 big water-smooth rocks,   (noun phrase)
      3 cedars along the bank and white birches,   (absolute)
   2 the logs warm in the sun,   (absolute)
      3 smooth to sit on,   (adjective phrase)

3 without bark,   (prepositional phrase)
3 gray to the touch;   (adjective phrase)
1 slowly the feeling of disappointment left him.   (base)

Now, using these densely textured sentences that result from adding levels of free modifiers, write a paragraph that has for its core the following ideas:

An open window. Many sounds come in. Some are harsh and some are gentle. Some blend with others; some remain separate and distinct.

4

Rhetoric of productive paragraphs

Introduction

Productive rhetoric attempts to clarify our understanding of both the sentence and the paragraph. It goes beyond those elementary definitions that regard a sentence as a group of words beginning with a capital and ending with some mark of punctuation and a paragraph as a group of sentences expressing a single idea. It demands more in its definition of a paragraph than the suggestion that a paragraph functions simply as a device for the reader's vision, a device that groups certain sentences and separates them from other sentences. To define a football field as "that which lies between the two goal lines" helps us to identify a football field, but not to understand its purpose. And, in a similar way, the above definitions help us to identify the basic units called sentences and paragraphs, but do not satisfy us as explanations. In short, they do not help us to understand why we group these words or these sentences together. But, before attempting to give new and meaningful definitions, let us take another look at sentence and paragraph construction.

From sentences to paragraphs

In dealing with the rhetoric of productive sentences, we worked with the two-level sentence, that which has a main or base clause as its first level and an added subordinate element, a free modifier, as its second level:

He roused himself and shifted, only to sink again in a sea of drowsiness and porter.
—James Boyd, *Drums*

1 He roused himself and shifted, (base)
  2 only to sink again in a sea of drowsiness and porter. (infinitive phrase)

One may move beyond the single added element (shown above) to a parallel series on the second level. The free modifiers added here produce a rich texture, and the parallelism here produces strong intra-T-unit coordination:

He acquired a half-section, free from debt, fertile, well-stocked, adorned with a cement silo, a chicken-run, a new windmill.
—Sinclair Lewis, "Young Man Axelbrod"

1 He acquired a half-section, (base)
  2 free from debt, (adjective phrase)
  2 fertile, (adjective)
  2 well-stocked, (participle)
  2 adorned with a cement silo, a chicken-run, a new windmill. (participial phrase)

Going beyond the parallel series on the second level (shown above), we arrive at the multi-level sentence, which is the result of adding several free modifier structures:

Each lower leg was a piston, a thousand pounds of white bone, sunk in thick ropes of muscle, sheathed over in a gleam of pebbled skin like the mail of a terrible warrior.
—Ray Bradbury, "A Sound of Thunder"

1 Each lower leg was a piston, (base)
  2 a thousand pounds of white bone, (appositive)
    3 sunk in thick ropes of muscle, (participial phrase)
      4 sheathed over in a gleam of pebbled skin like the mail of a terrible warrior. (participial phrase)

The following diagrams graphically illustrate the three relationships described above:

LEVEL TWO SENTENCE — BASE PLUS SINGLE ADDED ELEMENT

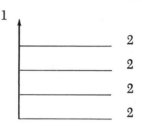

LEVEL TWO SENTENCE —
BASE PLUS PARALLEL SERIES OF LEVEL TWO STRUCTURES

MULTI-LEVEL SENTENCE —
BASE PLUS THREE ADDED ELEMENTS IN A PATTERN OF SUBORDINATION

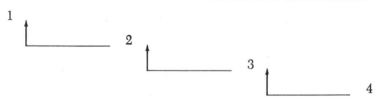

In all level two sentences, the second level elements communicate directly with the top level (level one). They do not need or depend on any other level two element that may happen to be present in the sentence. This pattern involves the use of *coordination*. In contrast, the subordinate levels in the multi-level sentences can only communicate with the top level through the added levels of free modifiers. This pattern uses *subordination*. The level four element in the Bradbury sentence keeps its relationship with the base clause and its meaning only by going through levels three and two. To by-pass levels two and three may produce a readable, logical sentence, but to do so distorts the relationships of words and phrases and the natural flow of the sentence originally intended by the author.

The structural relationships evident in the sentences above also appear in the paragraph. The principles of the rhetoric of the productive sentence also form the basis for the rhetoric of the productive paragraph. The addition of levels produces both direction and texture within a paragraph.

As with the rhetoric of the productive sentence, the use of a numbering system indicates the relationship between sentences within the paragraph. Number "1" marks the level one sentence, or the *top sentence*. It parallels the base clause of the sentence rhetoric. The construction of a top sentence plus one additional sentence, a level two, forms one of the most elementary paragraph patterns.

> This is a story about my father, and about God. Neither is very easy to understand.
>
> —John Neufeld, *Edgar Allan*

1 This is a story about my father, and about God.
  2 Neither is very easy to understand.

A writer may extend the above paragraph pattern and use a series of level two sentences. This coordination not only gives the necessary unity but also gives the paragraph both its direction and its richer texture:

> In this connection, we may observe, first, the phrase "brown study." It is not the "frosted flower," the "marmoreal immobility," or any one of a thousand such phrases which would aim for the pure effect. It is merely the brown study which astonishes—a phrase which denies, as it were, the finality of the situation, underplays the pathos, and merely reminds one of those moments of childish pensiveness into which the grown-up cannot penetrate. And the phrase itself is a cliché—the common now echoed in the uncommon.
>
> —Robert Penn Warren, "Pure and Impure Poetry"

1 In this connection, we may observe, first, the phrase "brown study."
  2 It is not the "frosted flower," the "marmoreal immobility," or any one of a thousand such phrases which would aim for the pure effect.
  2 It is merely the brown study which astonishes—a phrase which denies, as it were, the finality of the situation, underplays the pathos, and merely reminds one of those moments of childish pensiveness into which the grown-up cannot penetrate.

2 And the phrase itself is a cliché—the common now echoed in the uncommon.

A writer may also use the other pattern basic to sentences and paragraphs, that of subordination. Through the addition of sentences that move away from the top level of the paragraph, a writer produces a paragraph of the density and texture of the following:

"Guilt" is a strange word to have become associated with the experience of pleasure. It suggests, to begin with, that we have a deep conviction of time wasted, of life wasted, of worthwhile opportunities missed, whenever we indulge ourselves in a mild flirtation with leisure. There are valuable things we might be doing if we were not goldbricking just now; those valuable things might prove enormously useful to society, to our families, to our own souls; in goldbricking itself there is no value. We are either laborers in the vineyard or we are slackers in the shade.

—Walter Kerr, *The Decline of Pleasure*

1 "Guilt" is a strange word to have become associated with the experience of pleasure.
2 It suggests, to begin with, that we have a deep conviction of time wasted, of life wasted, of worthwhile opportunities missed, whenever we indulge ourselves in a mild flirtation with leisure.
3 There are valuable things we might be doing if we were not goldbricking just now; those valuable things might prove enormously useful to society, to our families, to our own souls; in goldbricking itself there is no value.
4 We are either laborers in the vineyard or we are slackers in the shade.

By crossing the two basic patterns, coordination and subordination, we arrive at a third pattern, "the *mixed sequence*," as Professor Christensen called it. The example below illustrates how a paragraph can use both coordination and subordination in "mixed sequence":

Syme had vanished. A morning came, and he was missing from work; a few thoughtless people commented on his absence. On the next day nobody mentioned him. On the third day Winston went into the vestibule of the Records Department to look at the notice board. One of the notices carried a printed list of the members of the Chess Committee, of whom Syme had been one. It looked almost exactly as it had looked before—nothing had been crossed out—but it was one name shorter. It was enough. Syme had ceased to exist; he had never existed.

—George Orwell, *1984*

1 Syme had vanished.

  2 A morning came, and he was missing from work; a few thoughtless people commented on his absence.

  2 On the next day nobody mentioned him.

  2 On the third day Winston went into the vestibule of the Records Department to look at the notice board.

    3 One of the notices carried a printed list of the members of the Chess Committee, of whom Syme had been one.

      4 It look almost exactly as it had looked before—nothing had been crossed out—but it was one name shorter.

      5 It was enough.

      6 Syme had ceased to exist; he had never existed.

Two other basic paragraph structures need to be illustrated. The first uses a transitional sentence at the opening of a paragraph. Such a sentence links two separate paragraphs and eases the shift from one topic, or part of a topic, to another. The second paragraph structure employs a sentence that functions as a conclusion in which writers frequently like to summarize what they have said in the paragraph. Sometimes, of course, their conclusions may require two sentences.

PARAGRAPH WITH TRANSITIONAL SENTENCE

At first, they did nothing more than confiscate rice hoarded in the more prosperous villages and drive off pigs and cows. But then the more ruthless began organizing into gangs. With a few picked men, the leader would go from village to village, threatening to destroy them if they did not enroll a certain number in his band. Within months, his force would run to several thousands and then he would settle down to real banditry.

—Ray Kerrison, *Bishop Walsh of Maryknoll*

T At first, they did nothing more than confiscate rice hoarded in the more prosperous villages and drive off pigs and cows.

1 But then the more ruthless began organizing into gangs.

2 With a few picked men, the leader would go from village to village, threatening to destroy them if they did not enroll a certain number in his band.

3 Within months, his force would run to several thousands and then he would settle down to real banditry.

PARAGRAPH WITH CONCLUSION

Hope alone is not enough. Meaningful hope has to be given implementation by installments. It is a mere mockery until a first down payment has been made in a substantial step toward truly equal education; then a further step toward fulfillment of promises must be made in the provision of housing worthy of American citizens. After that, meaningful hope will have to be translated into opportunities for employment on a higher and higher plane, less and less menial, and more and more professional. Life without hope is empty. But true hopes are illustrated hopes.

—Allan Nevins, "The Tradition of the Future"

1 Hope alone is not enough.

2 Meaningful hope has to be given implementation by installments.

3 It is a mere mockery until a first down payment has been made in a substantial step toward truly equal education; then a further step toward fulfillment of promises must be made in the provision of housing worthy of American citizens.

4 After that, meaningful hope will have to be translated into opportunities for employment on a higher and higher plane, less and less menial, and more and more professional.

C1 Life without hope is empty.

C2 But true hopes are illustrated hopes.

It should be clear that each of the paragraphs used in this chapter represents more than just a group of sentences relating to a single idea and that the paragraph itself represents more than a visual guide for the reader. Instead, a *paragraph* groups related sentences, not in a hodgepodge grouping, but in an arrangement meaningful because of the interrelation of its parts. According to Professor Christensen, a paragraph "is a sequence of structurally related sentences." If a group of structurally related sentences defines the paragraph, then a group of structurally related words defines the *sentence*. Sentences, like paragraphs, are not random groupings of words and phrases but have coherence because the words in the sentence relate to one another.

If the groupings of sentences that we write result in productive paragraphs in which the sentences relate structurally, then our writing would improve, simply because it would make more sense.

Exercises in analysis

Using the examples on page 72 for reference, diagram the paragraphs in the following three exercises. As in the case of the rhetoric of the sentence, these exercises order the paragraphs according to their difficulty, from the simple in Exercise One to the more complex in Exercise Three.

EXERCISE ONE

(1) The first group, "Questions about the text itself," calls for answers based on textual analysis. Its first part, "Questions of form," treats the text as if it were independent of its creator and its observer. The second, "Questions of rhetoric," focuses on matters that questions of form deliberately overlook—that is, the relationship of the piece of writing to the writer or speaker, to its setting, and to its audience. The third, "Questions about meaning," runs from those about a single word to those about the work taken as a whole.

> Commission on English, 1965, CEEB
> *Freedom and Discipline in English*

(2) Lastly, a whole new terminology, as ornately shoddy as the satin rayon casket liner, has been invented by the funeral industry to replace the direct and serviceable vocabu-

lary of former times. Undertaker has been supplanted by "funeral director" or "mortician." (Even the classified section of the telephone directory gives recognition to this; in its pages you will find "Undertakers—see Funeral Directors.") Coffins are "caskets"; hearses are "coaches," or "professional cars"; flowers are "floral tributes"; corpses generally are "loved ones," but mortuary etiquette dictates that a specific corpse be referred to by name only—as, "Mr. Jones"; cremated ashes are "cremains." Euphemisms such as "slumber room," "reposing room," and "calcination—the kindlier heat" abound in the funeral business.

—Jessica Mitford, *The American Way of Death*

(3) As he came near, what impressed me first was his clothes. He wore dark trousers of some serge material tucked into tall boots and held at the waist by a wide belt, both of a soft black leather tooled in intricate design. A coat of the same dark material as the trousers was neatly folded and strapped to his saddle-roll. His shirt was fine spun linen, rich brown in color. The handkerchief knotted loosely around his throat was black silk. His hat was not the familiar Stetson, not the familiar gray or muddy tan. It was plain black, soft in texture, unlike any hat I ever seen, with a creased crown and a wide curling brim swept down in front to shield the face.

—Jack Schaefer, *Shane*

(4) The great red hills stand desolate, and the earth has torn away like flesh. The lightning flashes over them, the clouds pour down upon them, the dead streams come to life, full of the red blood of the earth. Down in the valleys women scratch the soil that is left, and the maize hardly reaches the height of a man. They are valleys of old men and old women, of mothers and children. The men are away, the young men and girls are away. The soil cannot keep them any more.

—Alan Paton, *Cry, the Beloved Country*

EXERCISE TWO

(1) Twenty-five years ago, Howard Roark laughed. Standing naked at the edge of a cliff, his face gaunt, his hair the color of bright orange rind, his body a composition of straight, clean lines and angles, each curve breaking into smooth, clean planes, Howard Roark laughed. It was probably a soundless

laugh; most of Ayn Rand's heroes laugh soundlessly, particularly while making love. It was probably a laugh with head thrown back; most of Ayn Rand's heroes do things with their heads thrown back, particularly while dealing with the rest of mankind. It was probably a laugh that had a strange kind of simplicity; most of Ayn Rand's heroes act with a strange kind of simplicity, particularly when what they are doing is of a complex nature.

—Nora Ephron, "Strange Kind of Simplicity"

(2) McTeague remembered his mother, too, who, with the help of the Chinaman, cooked for forty miners. She was an overworked drudge, fiery and energetic for all that, filled with the one idea of having her son rise in life and enter a profession. The chance had come at last when the father died, corroded with alcohol, collapsing in a few hours. Two or three years later a travelling dentist visited the mine and put up his tent near the bunk-house. He was more or less a charlatan, but he fired Mrs. McTeague's ambition, and young McTeague went away with him to learn his profession. He had learnt it after a fashion, mostly by watching the charlatan operate. He had read many of the necessary books, but he was too hopelessly stupid to get much benefit from them.

—Frank Norris, McTeague

(3) When my father was admitted to the bar, he returned to Maycomb and began his practice. Maycomb, some twenty miles east of Finch's Landing, was the county seat of Maycomb County. Atticus's office in the courthouse contained little more than a hat rack, a spittoon, a checkerboard, and an unsullied code of Alabama. His first two clients were the last two persons hanged in the Maycomb county jail. Atticus had urged them to plead Guilty to second-degree murder and escape with their lives, but they were Haverfords, in Maycomb County a name synonymous with jackass. The Haverfords had dispatched Maycomb's leading blacksmith in a misunderstanding arising from the alleged wrongful detention of a mare, were imprudent enough to do it in the presence of three witnesses, and insisted that the son-of-a-bitch-had-it-coming-to-him was a good enough defense for anybody. They persisted in pleading Not Guilty to first-degree murder, so there was nothing much Atticus could do for his clients

except be present at their departure, an occasion that was probably the beginning of my father's profound distaste for the practice of criminal law.

—Harper Lee, *To Kill a Mockingbird*

(4) George felt himself urged from the room. The crash with which his father fell on the bed behind him was still in his ears as he fled. On the staircase, which he rushed down as if its steps were an inclined plane, he ran into his charwoman on her way up to do the morning cleaning of the room. "Jesus!" she cried, and covered her face with her apron, but he was already gone. Out of the front door he rushed, across the roadway, driven towards the water. Already he was grasping at the railings as a starving man clutches food. He swung himself over, like the distinguished gymnast he had once been in his youth, to his parents' pride. With weakening grip he was still holding on when he spied between the railings a motorbus coming which would easily cover the noise of his fall, called in a low voice: "Dear parents, I have always loved you, all the same," and let himself drop.

—Franz Kafka, "The Judgment"

EXERCISE THREE

(1) In later years, I confess that I do not envy the white boy as I once did. I have learned that success is to be measured not so much by the position that one has reached in life as by the obstacles which he has overcome while trying to succeed. Looked at from this standpoint, I almost reach the conclusion that often the Negro boy's birth and connection with an unpopular race is an advantage, so far as real life is concerned. With a few exceptions, the Negro youth must work harder and must perform his task even better than a white youth in order to secure recognition. But out of the hard and unusual struggle through which he is compelled to pass, he gets a strength, a confidence, that one misses whose pathway is comparatively smooth by reason of birth and race.

—Booker T. Washington, *Up from Slavery*

(2) I bowed in reply to his nod of dismissal and followed Christian to the ladderway. The berth was a screened-off space of the lower deck, on the larboard side, abreast of the main hatch. Its dimensions were scarcely more than eight feet

by ten, yet four of us were to make this kennel our home. Three or four boxes stood around the sides, and a scuttle of heavy discoloured glass admitted a dim light. A quadrant hung on a nail driven into the ship's side, and, though she was not long from Deptford, a reek of bilge water hung in the air. A handsome, sulky-looking boy of sixteen, in a uniform like my own, was arranging the gear in his box, and straightened up to give me a contemptuous stare. His name was Hayward, as I learned when Christian introduced us briefly, and he scarcely deigned to take my outstretched hand.

—Charles Nordhoff and James Norman Hall,
Mutiny on the Bounty

(3) I will describe the buildings: there is a large warehouse on the ground floor which is used as a store. The front door to the house is next to the warehouse door, and inside the front door is a second doorway which leads to a staircase. There is another door at the top of the stairs, with a frosted glass window in it, which has "Office" written in black letters across it. That is the large main office, very big, very light, and very full. Elli, Miep, and Mr. Koophuis work there in the daytime. A small dark room containing the safe, a wardrobe, and a large cupboard leads to a small somewhat dark second office. Mr. Kraler and Mr. Van Daan used to sit here, now it is only Mr. Kraler. One can reach Kraler's office from the passage, but only via a glass door which can be opened from the inside, but not easily from the outside.

—Anne Frank, *The Diary of a Young Girl*

(4) I am young, I am twenty years old; yet I know nothing of life but despair, death, fear, and fatuous superficiality cast over an abyss of sorrow. I see how peoples are set against one another, and in silence, unknowingly, foolishly, obediently, innocently slay one another. I see that the keenest brains of the world invent weapons and words to make it yet more refined and enduring. And all the men of my age, here and over there, throughout the whole world see these things; all my generation is experiencing these things with me. What would our fathers do if we suddenly stood up and came before them and proffered our account? What do they expect of us if a time ever comes when the war is over? Through the years our business has been killing; it was our first calling in

life. Our knowledge of life is limited to death. What will happen afterwards? And what shall come out of us?

—Erich Maria Remarque, *All Quiet on the Western Front*

Exercise in composition

Now that you have been exposed to some of the varieties of direction and effect possible in sentence construction, write a paragraph of your own, based on your reading and interpretation of the following ideas:

> The view from my living room window: autumn leaves of red, brown, gold. Dirt road on right, straight down hill to the general store, then sharp left turn out of sight behind clump of maples. Because of dry summer, low water in creek. Breeze, rustling dead leaves, the first feeling of winter not far away.
>
> —Robert L. Shurter and James M. Reid,
> *A Program for Effective Writing*

You should immediately notice that the information given here has a quiet, reminiscent quality about it, which should affect the tone of your paragraph. Concentrate especially on writing sequences of structurally related words and structurally related sentences.

5

Semantics as a factor in style

Introduction

Thus far we have looked at the criteria of mature style, at the arrangement of words, at the rhetoric of sentences and paragraphs. All of these factors, however, depend upon words, and words can elude us and baffle us more easily than we care to admit. We may find ourselves wondering about the function of words, like Alice, in this passage from *Through the Looking Glass:*

> "I don't know what you mean by 'glory,'" Alice said.
>
> Humpty Dumpty smiled contemptuously. "Of course you don't—till I tell you. I meant 'there's a nice knock-down argument for you!'"
>
> "But 'glory' doesn't mean 'a nice knock-down argument,'" Alice objected.
>
> "When I use a word," Humpty Dumpty said, in rather a scornful tone, "it means just what I choose it to mean—neither more nor less."
>
> "The question is," said Alice, "whether you can make words mean so many different things."
>
> "The question is," said Humpty Dumpty, "which is to be master—that's all."
>
> —Lewis Carroll, *Through the Looking Glass*

If words can represent or stand for whatever we wish, and if words can dominate us like tyrants, then we should seriously consider some of the aspects of *semantics, the study of the meanings and changes of meaning of words.* As a result, the complexities and consequences of using certain words or types of words will appear. Both the narrowing and the expanding of the meaning of words become factors in a writing style.

Lesson one — tone

Of the many factors that contribute to a writer's style, the most personal seems to be the selection of the words, or combinations of words, that say exactly what the writer wishes to say. That the numbers of words at our disposal escape comprehension suggests the vast possibilities for individuality. For example, the following words are only some of the possible synonyms for the word "leap":

> jump, vault, spring, hop, bound, bounce, upleap, upspring, updive, jump over, overleap, overjump, overskip, hurdle, clear, negotiate, leapfrog, curvet, capriole, buck, buckjump, start, start up, start aside, pounce, pounce on or upon, hippety-hop °

Each of these synonyms carries its own shade of meaning, its own interpretation of the idea of "leap." The writer creates the particular *tone or attitude* he wants by carefully choosing a word or words to suggest that attitude or shade of meaning.

Exercise in synonyms

Too often we restrict ourselves to a few overused words, failing to tap the tremendous word resources available to us. To again see the possibilities, take the five following terms and supply as many synonyms as possible:

1. big (adj.)
2. swiftly (adv.)
3. sad (adj.)
4. walk (verb)
5. house (noun)

° *Roget's International Thesaurus* (Thomas Y. Crowell Company, New York, 1962), p. 189.

Besides having synonyms, words have meanings of two kinds—denotative and connotative. *Denotation refers to the exact meaning or the dictionary meaning of a word. Connotation refers to the attitudes, feelings, and emotions that a word suggests or implies to a reader.* For example, the words "offer" and "deal" both reflect the idea of a business proposal; however, "deal" often suggests something shady or underhanded.

Professionals in every area of the writing world, whether it be fiction, nonfiction, advertising copy, political speeches, or journalism, know and depend on the enormous power of words. They know that some words have a general meaning or connotation, one shared by many people; they know that other words have a personal meaning or connotation, one often differing from person to person. They know, too, that connotation has a great deal to do with tone, and that the attitude of a writing, a speech, or an advertisement may have a positive, neutral, or negative connotation.

As a result, writers select a vocabulary that suggests whatever they intend. They may say "slender" or "skinny," "proud" or "arrogant," "inexpensive" or "cheap," or "public servant" or "bureaucrat." Each creates its own picture.

Obviously, the images words create do not necessarily have to be true and complete images. Manipulation of words causes us to accept or reject a literary character, a historical figure, a commercial product, a political candidate, a news event.

Too often, words improperly used can result in the destruction of a reputation. Witch hunts illustrate the force of unfavorable connotations of words. Many Puritans of the late seventeenth century reacted irrationally to the term "witch" and many Americans of the early 1950's reacted similarly to the word "Commie." On the other hand, some words abound with favorable connotations. Words like "freedom," "liberty," "democracy," "mother," and "Christmas" have a positive quality about them. Nevertheless, writers can abuse these words too, most often by using them as a smoke screen to hide something less savory.

Since people bring their own experiences to words, their reactions to language will vary. Writers, then, to some degree, expose themselves to an unknown quantity, for they may not know how their audience will respond. They must realize that meanings of words change and therefore connotations change. The word "fat" once associated with jolly Old St. Nick, or Friar Tuck, now unpleasantly suggests the overweight person; the word "spinster," formerly a woman who spins, now unpleasantly suggests a lonely, unmarried female.

Exercise in analysis

March 9: "The monster has escaped from the place of his banishment. ..."

March 10: "The Corsican ogre has landed at Cape Juan."

March 11: "The tiger has shown himself at Gap. The troops are advancing on all sides to arrest his progress. He will conclude his miserable adventure by becoming a wanderer among the mountains. ..."

March 12: "The monster has actually advanced as far as Grenoble."

March 13: "The tyrant is now at Lyons. Fear and terror seized all at his appearance."

March 18: "The usurper has ventured to approach to within 60 hours' march of the capital."

March 19: "Bonaparte is advancing by forced marches, but it is impossible he can reach Paris."

March 20: "Napoleon will arrive under the walls of Paris tomorrow."

March 21: "The Emperor Napoleon is at Fontainebleau."

March 22: "Yesterday evening His Majesty The Emperor made his public entry and arrived at the Tuileries. Nothing can exceed the universal joy."

The Moniteur, March 1815

These actual selections from the official journal of the French government for the year 1815 illustrate two of the many pitfalls involved in writing. First, it shows the careless use of fact and opinion. Second, it reveals the paper's change in policy by employing connotative words.

During the two weeks when Napoleon approached Paris and regained power, what connotative words did the paper use? How did those words change as the official climate in Paris changed?

Exercise in composition

The following, a paragraph from Eric Sevareid's editorial "Dirt, Grime, and Cruel Crowding," gives a very unfavorable view of modern city life:

Today, the ugly office skyscrapers go up, shops and graceful homes are obliterated, their inhabitants forced away, and
year after year New Yorkers step around the pits, . . . breathe
the fine mist of dust, absorb the hammering noise night and
day, and telephone in vain for carpenter or plumber.

Rewrite this paragraph in such a manner as to create a more
favorable or positive impression of life in New York. The careful
substitution of words and the careful addition of modifiers should
be sufficient to produce the desired effect.

Lesson two — euphemisms

. . . Our word *euphemism* is derived from the Greek *eu*,
meaning "well" and *phanai*, "to speak"; the Greek word *eu-
phēmizein* meant "to use fair words, or words of good omen."
Now, however, euphemism is a term applied to a mild, sooth-
ing, usually vague expression that is substituted for a precise,
or blunt, or less agreeable term. It is a linguistic device, by
which people avoid talking about, and often thinking about,
unpleasant realities.

. . .

There are, of course, certain social and conversational situations in which euphemisms may be desirable. For example,
good judgment would suggest saying "plant food" if the person to whom one is talking considers "manure" a shocking
word; and tact and kindness might recommend "he passed
away" or some other euphemism for death in conversation
with one recently bereaved. But increasingly in modern writing euphemisms are rejected because they are roundabout, in-
exact, hesitant, and weak. Like other vague terms and circumlocutions, they carry the reader away from, instead of
bringing him close to the real meaning. In general, they
should be used only when a situation involving personal feelings demands a delicate avoidance of fact. Normally the blunt
factual term should be used because it is more precise and
emphatic.

—Newman P. Birk and Genevieve B. Birk,
Understanding and Using English

Pleasant or impressive names for unpleasant or trivial things are known as euphemisms. The most common motive of such verbal upgrading is the speaker's or writer's desire to seem dignified or refined. The most familiar euphemisms are those for elementary facts of human existence. . . .

. . .

The practice of using euphemisms to avoid the repetition of more unpretentious words is often called *elegant variation.* A writer describing the habits of the swordfish will rightly feel that repeating the name of the fish in every second sentence would be monotonous. However, his writing will sound strained if he starts using circumlocutions like "scaled creature," "aquatic marauder," "denizen of the deep," and "knight of the brine."

—Hans P. Guth, *Words and Ideas*

As these definitions show, euphemisms have become very much a part of semantics. But, while euphemisms may allow us to say something unpleasant in a more pleasant manner, they also may cause us to miss saying what we intended to say. As writers, then, we must use our own judgment as to when and when not to use euphemisms.

Exercise

Make a list of euphemisms. The above definitions will serve as a beginning and will also suggest the areas where euphemisms have been traditionally used.

Exercise in composition

Work with the following situation:

Two persons (both male or both female or one of each) in a pit. Too deep to get out. They discuss their plight.

To present the conversation, use any literary vehicle—straight dialogue, short story, drama, poetry, song, whatever—but deliberately overload it with euphemisms. You may consult the list in Appendix A. Focus on the two persons in the pit without worrying about how they got there.

Lesson three — clichés

One of the most interesting things about our language, and most especially our American brand of English, is that its vocabulary is constantly changing. Whenever the need arises, new words appear, and others, no longer needed, or no longer in fashion, die out. One notable exception is a certain group of words that seem to remain because they have become a sort of informal code in our efforts to communicate. When this occurs, these overused words generally find themselves in that company called *cliché*.

The term *cliché* derives from the French term for stereotype, a one-piece printing plate. From this we get the idea of set form, an idea easily transferable from printing to language. Today, then, cliché means *a word or phrase so overused that its freshness and originality have disappeared;* it becomes a set word or set phrase, never changing and never really carrying anything new in the way of meaning.

Clichés have also been labeled "worn-out similes," "tired metaphors," "trite expressions," "bromides," and "hackneyed expressions." The definition of "bromide" helps further in explaining the cliché. *Bromide* literally means a sedative or medicine to calm nervousness and to cause sleep; and clichés tend to do exactly that. Since they require no effort to use, and since they do not force the writer to think, they lull a person into a lethargic state of noncreativity, and, finally, nonthinking.

The fact that we have so many clichés in our language indicates a strain of laziness that runs through us all. In thinking, in speaking, and in writing, we too often turn to the stock expression instead of tapping the tremendous inventive possibilities of our language. Because it represents this laziness, we should avoid the cliché, or as someone has called it, "echo talk." This label fits well; the cliché represents a hollow echo, not the original voice, not the original word. Such use of echoes leads to "echo thinking"—hollow, shallow thinking, nothing more than the parroting of tired language. If avoiding clichés helps to avoid "echo thinking," then we should avoid clichés for that reason alone.

Exercise in analysis

Numerous pieces have been written to illustrate the deadly effects of the cliché on writing and on speaking. Frank Sullivan's series featuring the "cliché expert" represents the best known of these. But the sample below, from another source, serves equally well.

All's Trite with the World

SYDNEY J. HARRIS

My friend, whom we will call Sandy, because that is not his name, works for a newspaper in a Midwestern city that shall also be anonymous. Sandy is employed as a feature writer, and his editors are (I assume) quite proud of his literary abilities.

Sandy specializes in Poignant stories. He can be Sad at a moment's notice. He particularly likes to write about little girls who have lost their dogs and the old ladies wandering alone in the big city. Touching.

The readers go for Sandy's vibrant prose, because he is never at a loss for a word or a phrase. He puts things so beautifully and so simply that even a sixth-grader can understand him and marvel at his verbal powers.

For instance, when someone's child dies, Sandy knows it leaves an Aching Void in the parents' lives. They also face Blank Despair at this tragedy that struck them like a Bolt from the Blue. Life, as Sandy loves to repeat, is no Bed of Roses.

Oh, Sandy is a whiz with words. He knows all about the things that are put to the Acid Test and the men who see these things through to the Bitter End. He also knows that every man has his Achilles' Heel, even Captains of Industry, Gay Lotharios, Good Samaritans, and Social Butterflies.

Sometimes the editors set Sandy loose on a juicy crime, and then how vividly he tells of the Blunt Instrument, the bandits Armed to the Teeth, the police Spreading a Dragnet, and later the convict whose Doom is Sealed. Sometimes the convict walks the Last Mile Sneering at the Grim Reaper.

Why, you could go right through Sandy's stories and pick out these little gems of expression in every paragraph. Take the Battle Royal, the Crack of Doom, the Fly in the Ointment, the Eternal Triangle, the Errand of Mercy, the Wry Jest, the Dog's Life, the Gala Event, and lots more just as good.

In Sandy's world, people are never merely ignorant; they are Blissfully Ignorant. They are not in earnest, but in Deadly Earnest. Sometimes they are Conspicuous by Their Absence, while others Beat around the Bush, and Disaster Overtakes Them at One Fell Swoop. Last but Not Least, that is.

You can see why Sandy is such a valuable man. His appeal is universal; it reaches down into the Nethermost Depths of Humanity. Even a moron can understand him.

List the clichés you find in the Harris paragraphs.

Exercise in composition

Occasionally, to make his point a writer must use the cliché. The present assignment presents you with such an opportunity. It will give you a chance to have some fun with clichés and to make fun of those whose writing has not advanced much beyond the trite.

Using as many clichés as possible, in fact overusing them as much as possible, put together a version of some radio or TV program that demonstrates a reliance on such expressions. Write it in play form, script form, short-story form—whatever one most effectively conveys your ideas. A list of clichés appears in Appendix B.

Lesson four — similes and metaphors

Lesson Three deals with clichés, those dead words and phrases still walking around, the zombies of our language. The juxtaposition of this lesson with Lesson Four, which deals with living words and phrases, should emphasize the strengths of similes and metaphors and, at the same time, the weaknesses of clichés.

Both similes and metaphors function as comparisons between unlike objects that share some similarity or similarities. The simile uses "like" or "as" in its comparison; the metaphor does not. These examples illustrate this difference:

Life goes on forever like the gnawing of a mouse.
—Edna St. Vincent Millay, "Ashes of Life"

Life is mostly froth and bubble.
—A. L. Gordon, "Ye Wearie Wayfarer"

Both examples compare—one compares the span of life to the continuous gnawing of a mouse; the other compares life to an elusive and deceptive phenomenon. The first uses "like"; the second does not. In each case, the writer changes the meaning of the word "life" for us, enlarging our view of an abstraction.

Exercise in analysis

For each of the examples below, determine the following:

a. every simile and/or metaphor
b. what comparison the writer makes

(1)   He waved a kindly hand to his supporters, and bowed in a regal sort of manner, rather like an Eastern monarch acknowledging the plaudits of the mob.
—P. G. Wodehouse, "Jeeves and the Song of Songs"

(2)   ... the black flower of civilized society—a prison.
—Nathaniel Hawthorne, *The Scarlet Letter*

(3)   And continuing to mumble something which they could no longer catch, he disappeared into the darkness between the sparsely placed oil-lamps, like one losing his way in the bowels of the earth.
—Pär Lagerkvist, *Barabbas*

(4)   "John [Sir John Gielgud] is claret," as a wine-loving English critic once put it. "And Larry [Sir Laurence Olivier] is Burgundy."
—Kenneth Tynan,
"In His Talent, Shakespeare Summoned Up"

(5)   When the sunrays at last struck full and mellowingly upon the earth, the youth saw that the landscape was streaked with two long, thin, black columns which disappeared on the brow of a hill in front and rearward vanished in a wood. They were like two serpents crawling from the cavern of the night.
—Stephen Crane, *The Red Badge of Courage*

(6)   And soon God had not just sent his Apostle, but had come himself, in a Cadillac, to make sure everything was all right no matter how much she worked and sinned, no matter the children she had lost; Daddy Faith, who was the King of Glory, Wonderful, Counsellor, the Mighty God, the Everlasting Father, the Prince of Peace.

—William Styron, *Lie Down in Darkness*

(7)   In a few years her body would be fullblown like a rose with loosened petals, but now the soft roundness was controlled and disciplined by sport.

—Carson McCullers, *Reflections in a Golden Eye*

(8)   Then the car turned away from the plains of Hattin and into a flat field where a burst of scarlet hit their eyes. The field was a red carpet of wild flowers.

—Leon Uris, *Exodus*

(9)   Bats flew silently through the air above, like hideous creatures in a dream.

—Pierre Loti, *An Iceland Fisherman*

(10)   The American spring is very much like spring anywhere—lively green fingers of things poking their way up through the dull and barren ground, the sudden surprise of tulips, the great, quiet explosion of apple blossoms.

—Robert Creamer, "First Pitch"

(11)   It was more than breathtaking, it was like having stumbled upon some alien cathedral on some other planet, which some otherworld race with their incomprehensible architecture and alien sculpture had ages past built, decorated and dedicated to their unknowable God.

—James Jones, *Go to the Widow-maker*

(12)   Over them all, over the clear light of the aspens and mountain ash, over the leaping flames of sumac and the hellfire flickerings of poison ivy, over the warpaint of the many oaks, rise the colors of one tree—the sugar maple—in the shout of a great army.

—Donald Culross Peattie, *A Natural History of Trees*

(13)   "Martha's father expects his . . . staff . . . to cling to the walls of this place, like the ivy. . . ."

—Edward Albee, *Who's Afraid of Virginia Woolf?*

(14) "This whole world is nothing but a big rat trap. All the good things that are offered you are nothing but cheese rinds and bits of pork, set out to drag a poor fellow into trouble."

—Selma Lagerlöf, "The Rat Trap"

(15) "He flunked the subject, and laid down and died like a hammer hit him!"

—Arthur Miller, *Death of a Salesman*

(16) Though he was a churchgoer by habit, the true god of that man was Money—red gold, shining silver, dull copper—the trinity that he worshiped in degree.

—Maurice Walsh, "The Quiet Man"

(17) Seen like this from above, the rows of colorful tented cabanas stretched out like the wings of a giant bird that had settled over the yellow sand.

—Irving Wallace, *The Plot*

(18) Life's but a walking shadow, a poor player
That struts and frets his hour upon the stage
And then is heard no more. It is a tale
Told by an idiot, full of sound and fury,
Signifying nothing.

—William Shakespeare, *Macbeth*

(19) The summer came upon the country like a conqueror.
—W. Somerset Maugham, *Of Human Bondage*

(20) It smelled like fifty million dead cigars.
—J. D. Salinger, *Catcher in the Rye*

The mixed metaphor

Like all language devices, the metaphor can and has been misused. An inexperienced writer may lose control of his imagery and create not a forceful comparison but a *mixed metaphor, the combination of two or more incongruous or illogical metaphors.* The writer begins with one metaphor, such as:

The highway of life is

To this the writer, experienced or inexperienced, must add an image in keeping with the comparison of life to a highway. He may add this:

The highway of life is a choppy sea.

However, the result, a mixed metaphor, moves away from the highway image to a new and different image dealing with the sea, certainly not in keeping with the original idea. The writer should have done something like this:

The highway of life is paved with cobblestones.

In this case, the two images complement one another, successfully suggesting the bumpiness of life.

What mixed metaphors do the examples below contain? How can we eliminate the problem in each of the following?

a. The British lion will never be a quiet lamb.
b. Like a porcupine, he bristled when he saw me and pulled in his horns.
c. The story of life is a sea of troubles.
d. If we are to reach the top of the ladder while we swim the river of life, we must keep our shoulder to the wheel.

Although writers should avoid the mixed metaphor, sometimes it has effective uses. The very oddity of it can draw our attention and may well create the effect the writer wanted. For example, this statement attributed to Samuel Goldwyn:

"They're always biting the hand that lays the golden egg."

Or this from James Branch Cabell's *Jurgen:*

"Indeed, it is a sad thing, Sylvia, to be murdered by the hand which, so to speak, is sworn to keep an eye on your welfare, and which rightfully should serve you on its knees."

This mixed metaphor recalls the double duty, as subject-kinsman and as host, of Shakespeare's Macbeth: his hand must keep an eye on Duncan's well-being.

Exercise in composition

The surf at such moments is not to be trifled with. In fact you never trifle with the surf; when it is in a playful mood, the surf trifles with you. That's the joy of swimming in it.

Along comes a large playful wave. It rises up and smacks you, shoves you along, knocks you off your feet like a big clumsy dog trying to ingratiate itself with a child. You are the child. It doesn't matter if you hold an Olympic gold medal; in the surf you wallow and are knocked around like any dog-paddler.

Another wave swells up, growing more intimidating by the moment. As it nears you, the great crest breaks, an immense amount of rushing water is about to crash over your head. You are just a morsel of flotsam, but you happen to be human and you have the ingenuity which raised your ancestors out of the water in the first place. You put your arms in front of you, your head between them, and dive through the wave. Despite its tremendous force, it hurtles harmlessly over you and smashes its energy ineffectually against the shore.

—John Knowles, "Everybody's Sport"

Knowles's excellent use of the simile and the metaphor not only adds to his description, but also dramatizes his comments about man's relationship to the sea.

Keeping in mind the effects that properly used similes and metaphors can have, write a paragraph with several comparisons in it. Use the following material as the core and expand its ideas into a well-written paragraph.

A deserted beach. The sun is setting. There is garbage on the beach. Seagulls on the beach look for scraps. Footprints in the sand from the people who were there earlier. Darkness comes.

Lesson five — allusions

... I was myself excited somewhat even as if they had been men. The more you think of it, the less the difference. And certainly there is not the fight recorded in Concord history, at least, if in the history of America, that will bear a moment's comparison with this, whether for the numbers engaged in it, or for the patriotism and heroism displayed. For numbers and for carnage it was an Austerlitz or Dresden.

Concord Fight! Two killed on the patriots' side, and Luther Blanchard wounded! Why here every ant was a Buttrick—"Fire, for God's sake Fire!"—and thousands shared the fate of Davis and Hosmer. There was not one hireling there. I have no doubt that it was a principle they fought for, as much as our ancestors, and not to avoid a three-penny tax on their tea; and the results of this battle will be as important and memorable to those whom it concerns as those of the battle of Bunker Hill, at least.

—Henry David Thoreau, *Walden*

The above portion of a Thoreau paragraph, even when taken out of context, illustrates expert use of the device known as the *allusion*. An allusion simply means *a reference to someone or something*. Thoreau's use of allusions allows him to reinforce and to dramatize what he has to say. He alludes or refers to battles in two great conflicts; he assumes the reader connects the bloody battles of Austerlitz and Dresden with the Napoleonic Wars and the battles of Concord and Bunker Hill with the American Revolution. Further, he assumes the reader knows of Buttrick, the leader of the Colonial forces at Concord, and of Davis and Hosmer, the first American casualties of the Revolution. The reader, knowing this sort of historical information about certain human conflicts, can better appreciate the levels of destruction that Thoreau has described in the battle of the ants.

In addition, we should note here that Thoreau does not stop to explain his allusions. If the reader fails to understand the allusions, what problems result?

Our speech and our writing, rich in allusions, contain references to the Bible, to classical literature, to history, and to many other areas as well. These allusions, not mere decorations, clarify important ideas, express vital points, or carry the desired tone or attitude of the author. The skillful writer weaves them into the texture of his work. Thoreau's allusions allow him to emphasize the ferocity of the struggle between the black and the red ants.

Writers must assume their readers recognize an allusion or understand a reference without any further identification. To stop and explain allusions would break up and destroy the flow and continuity of the writing. On the other hand, the author must be aware of the experience of his audience and judge the suitability of his allusions accordingly. The reason for using allusions should not be simple affectation but, rather, effective communication. If we do not understand the writer, the neatness of his allusions have little value. When correctly used, the allusion acts like a signal of mutual understanding, and a personal bond is immediately established between reader and writer.

Allusions, like metaphors, can lose their power through overuse. Tired references to "his Waterloo," "a Trojan horse," and "the sword of Damocles" have simply been worked to death. And extensive overuse produces clichés, such as "an Achilles' heel," "a gay Lothario," "a good Samaritan," and "the Grim Reaper."

Exercise in analysis

What allusions do the models below contain?

(1) Translators of poetry are the John Aldens of literature. They may woo the reader in another's name but, ultimately, they must speak for themselves—with translations that stand up in their own right as good poetry.

"Stuffed Eagle," *Time*

(2) And as its crowning symbol, it developed a radically new outlook on human destiny, which saw the meaning of history in terms of the progress of the human mind, and held that human history could be made to follow the direction that men choose to give it. Prometheus was the first modern.

—Charles Frankel, "The Revolution of Modernity"

(3) As if there were not already enough grim echoes of Dallas and Parkland Hospital, the scene at Central Receiving was degraded by human perversity.

"A Life on the Way to Death," *Time*

(4) The ultimate Orwellian nightmare in the electronic age is the telegenic candidate whose principal assets are a collar-ad profile and a toothpaste smile.

—Penn Kimball, "The Politics of Style"
Saturday Review

(5) And she could imitate him too, his way of talking, his nervous habits with his hands, his Gladstone pose.

—Walter Van Tilburg Clark,
The Ox-bow Incident

(6)   With this vignette of life on the brink in Washington, two able, young reporters, David Kraslow . . . and Stuart H. Loory . . . open up a Pandora's box of once locked-up secrets of State. What comes flying up out of the box is a tangle of red tapes that have strangled the hopes for peace and are responsible for the wrecked lives of millions of people. . . .

—David Schoenbrun, "Behind the Credibility Gap," *New York Times Book Review*

(7)   In charge of the editorial department there is often a democratic Dr. Jekyll—a propagandist who would be very happy to prove that John Dewey had been right about the ability of human nature to respond to truth and reason. But this worthy man controls only part of the machinery of mass communication. In charge of advertising we find an anti-democratic, because anti-rational, Mr. Hyde—or rather a Dr. Hyde, for Hyde is now a Ph.D. in psychology and has a master's degree as well in the social sciences. This Dr. Hyde would be very unhappy indeed if everybody always lived up to John Dewey's faith in human nature. Truth and reason are Jekyll's affair, not his.

—Aldous Huxley, *Brave New World Revisited*

Exercise in composition

A three-step procedure will help us construct sentences containing allusions:

Step One.   From the list of twenty potential allusions below, identify as many as possible. If some of the list remains unidentified, then try to find the kind of situation in which one might use them by consulting a reference book.

Step Two.   Practice writing some sentences containing allusions of your own and have someone else check them to see if you are using each allusion correctly.

Step Three.   After this practice, select any three allusions from the list of twenty and construct three separate sentences, ones of twenty or thirty words, containing those allusions.

Hobson's choice	Pandora's box
Pyrrhic victory	Captain Queeg

Cassandra	an Orwellian nightmare
a Frankenstein monster	Dr. Jekyll and Mr. Hyde
Scrooge	Job
Penelope	Jack Ketch
in this Gomorrah	Midas touch
Xanthippe	Damon and Pythias
Old Nick	Beau Brummell
John Barleycorn	Uriah Heep

6

Evaluating a writer's style

Introduction

This project invites a serious perusal of a single writing by a professional writer. The literary work need not be read to be studied. The investigation and evaluation involve discovering the writer's relationship to the factors dealt with in the five previous chapters of this text.

Exercise in evaluation

Use the following general steps and information to complete the evaluation:

Step One. Consider literary works that offer possibilities for investigation. A writer not known for his skill defeats the evaluation; a writer known for his writing abilities simplifies the evaluation.

Step Two. Select one writer and one of his literary works. The selection need not necessarily be read to be investigated, but a work already read has advantages.

Step Three. Inform the instructor of the choice. Each student will investigate his own selection; no two will evaluate the same work.

Step Four. Investigate and evaluate the work in the following areas:

a. factors of mature style
b. syntactic structures
c. rhetoric of productive sentences
d. rhetoric of productive paragraphs
e. semantic structures

Step Five. The samplings used for statistical studies need to be extensive enough to provide valid and conclusive results.

Step Six. The examples used to illustrate the different syntactic structures should represent the best of the author's writing. Therefore, select the examples carefully. To illustrate the author's wide creative abilities, employ as many different examples as possible and avoid repetition as much as possible.

Step Seven. Use the sample evaluation that follows as a guide and pattern for individual investigations.

Sample evaluation

On the next several pages you will find Thoreau's famous essay "On the Duty of Civil Disobedience," which he wrote in 1847 after spending a night in jail for refusing to pay a poll tax. This essay seems an excellent test case for any attempt to assess—using the criteria discussed in this book—the maturity of a writer's style. For, although written over a century ago in a style of writing seldom used today, the complex problems and ideas that Thoreau describes seem to have their analogues in our own day. And, in essence, a maturity of style is the ability to communicate facts and ideas effectively. If Thoreau does this, how he does it, and to what degree he uses the elements that this book suggests are the criteria for a mature style, are the subject of the sample evaluation that follows the essay.

On the Duty of Civil Disobedience

HENRY DAVID THOREAU

I heartily accept the motto,—"That government is best which governs least;" and I should like to see it acted up to more rapidly and systematically. Carried out, it finally amounts to this, which also I believe,—"That government is best which governs not at all;" and when men are prepared for it, that will be the kind of government which they will have. Government is at best but an expedient; but most governments are usually, and all governments are sometimes, inexpedient. The objections which have been brought against a standing army, and they are many and weighty, and deserve to prevail, may also at last be brought against a standing government. The standing army is only an arm of the standing government. The government itself, which is only the mode which the people have chosen to execute their will, is equally liable to be abused and perverted before the people can act through it. Witness the present Mexican war, the work of comparatively a few individuals using the standing government as their tool; for, in the outset, the people would not have consented to this measure.

This American government,—what is it but a tradition, though a recent one, endeavoring to transmit itself unimpaired to posterity, but each instant losing some of its integrity? It has not the vitality and force of a single living man; for a single man can bend it to his will. It is a sort of wooden gun to the people themselves; and, if ever they should use it in earnest as a real one against each other, it will surely split. But it is not the less necessary for this; for the people must have some complicated machinery or other, and hear its din, to satisfy that idea of government which they have. Governments show thus how successfully men can be imposed on, even impose on themselves, for their own advantage. It is excellent, we must all allow; yet this government never of itself furthered any enterprise, but by the alacrity with which it got out of its way. *It* does not keep the country free. *It* does not settle the West. *It* does not educate. The character inherent in the American people has done all that has been accomplished; and it would have done somewhat more, if the government had not sometimes got in its way. For government is an expedient by which men would fain succeed in letting one another alone; and, as has been said, when it is most expedient, the governed are most let alone by it. Trade and commerce, if they were not made of India rubber, would never manage to bounce over the obstacles which legislators are continually putting in their way; and, if one were to judge these men wholly by the effects of their actions, and not partly by their intentions, they would deserve to be classed and punished with those mischievous persons who put obstructions on the railroads.

But, to speak practically and as a citizen, unlike those who call themselves no-government men, I ask for, not at once no government, but *at once* a better government. Let every man make known what kind of government would command his respect, and that will be one step toward obtaining it.

After all, the practical reason why, when the power is once in the hands of the people, a majority are permitted, and for a long period continue, to rule, is not because they are most likely to be in the right, nor because this seems fairest to the minority, but because they are physically the strongest. But a government in which the majority rule in all cases cannot be based on justice, even as far as men understand it. Can there not be a government in which majorities do not virtually decide right and wrong, but conscience?—in which majorities decide only those questions to which the rule of expediency is applicable? Must the citizen ever for a moment, or in the least degree, resign his conscience, to the legislator? Why has every man a conscience, then? I think that we should be men first, and subjects afterward. It is not desirable to cultivate a respect for the law, so much as for the right. The only obligation which I have a right to assume, is to do at any time what I think right. It is truly enough said, that a corporation has no conscience; but a corporation of conscientious men is a corporation *with* a conscience. Law never made men a whit more just; and, by means of their respect for it, even the well-disposed are daily made the agents of injustice. A common and natural result of an undue respect for law is, that you may see a file of soldiers, colonel, captain, corporal, privates, powder-monkeys and all, marching in admirable order over hill and dale to the wars, against their wills, aye, against their common sense and consciences, which makes it very steep marching indeed, and produces a palpitation of the heart. They have no doubt that it is a damnable business in which they are concerned; they are all peaceably inclined. Now, what are they? Men at all? or small moveable forts and magazines, at the service of some unscrupulous man in power? Visit the Navy Yard, and behold a marine, such a man as an American government can make, or such as it can make a man with its black arts, a mere shadow and reminiscence of humanity, a man laid out alive and standing, and already, as one may say, buried under arms with funeral accompaniments, though it may be

"Not a drum was heard, nor a funeral note,
    As his corse to the ramparts we hurried;
Not a soldier discharged his farewell shot
    O'er the grave where our hero we buried."

The mass of men serve the State thus, not as men mainly, but as machines, with their bodies. They are the standing army, and the militia, jailers, constables, *posse comitatus*, &c. In most cases there is no free exercise whatever of the judgment or of the moral sense; but they put themselves on a level with wood and earth and stones; and wooden men can perhaps be manufactured that will serve the purpose as well. Such command no more respect than men of straw, or a lump of dirt. They have the same sort of worth only as horses and dogs. Yet such as these even are commonly esteemed good citizens. Others, as most legislators, politicians, lawyers, ministers, and office-holders, serve the State chiefly with their heads; and, as they rarely make any moral distinctions, they are as likely to serve the devil, without intending it, as God. A very few, as heroes, patriots, martyrs, reformers in the great sense, and *men*, serve the State with their consciences also, and so necessarily resist it for the most part; and they are commonly treated by it as enemies. A wise man will only be useful as a man, and will not submit to be "clay," and "stop a hole to keep the wind away," but leave that office to his dust at least:—

"I am too high-born to be propertied,
    To be a secondary at control,
    Or useful serving-man and instrument
    To any sovereign state throughout the world."

He who gives himself entirely to his fellow-men appears to them useless and selfish; but he who gives himself partially to them is pronounced a benefactor and philanthropist.

How does it become a man to behave toward this American government to-day? I answer that he cannot without disgrace be associated with it. I cannot for an instant recognize that political organization as *my* government which is the *slave's* government also.

All men recognize the right of revolution; that is, the right to refuse allegiance to and to resist the government, when its tyranny or its inefficiency are great and unendurable. But almost all say that such is not the case now. But such was the case, they think, in the Revolution of '75. If one were to tell me that this was a bad government because it taxed certain foreign commodities brought to its ports, it is most probable that I should not make an ado about it, for I can do without them: all machines have their friction; and possibly this does enough good to counterbalance the evil. At any rate, it is a great evil to make a stir about it. But when the friction comes to have its machine, and oppression and robbery are organized, I say, let us not have such a machine any longer. In other words, when a sixth of the population of a nation which has undertaken to be the refuge of liberty are slaves, and a whole country is unjustly overrun and conquered by a foreign army, and subjected to military law, I think that it is not too soon for honest men to rebel and revolutionize. What makes this duty the more urgent is the fact, that the country so overrun is not our own, but ours is the invading army.

Paley, a common authority with many on moral questions, in his chapter on the "Duty of Submission to Civil Government," resolves all civil obligation into expediency; and he proceeds to say, "that so long as the interest of the whole society requires it, that is, so long as the established government cannot be resisted or changed without public inconveniency, it is the will of God, that the established government be obeyed,—and no longer. This principle being admitted, the justice of every particular case of resistance is reduced to a computation of the quantity of the danger and grievance on the one side, and of the probability and expense of redressing it on the other." Of this, he says, every man shall judge for himself. But Paley appears never to have contemplated those cases to which the rule of expediency does not apply, in which a people, as well as an individual, must do justice, cost what it may. If I have unjustly wrested a plank from a drowning man, I must restore it to him though I drown myself. This, according to Paley, would be inconvenient. But he that would save his life, in such a case, shall lose it. This people must cease to hold slaves, and to make war on Mexico, though it cost them their existence as a people.

In their practice, nations agree with Paley; but does any one think that Massachusetts does exactly what is right at the present crisis?

"A drab of state, a cloth-o'-silver slut,
    To have her train borne up, and her soul trail in the dirt."

Practically speaking, the opponents to a reform in Massachusetts are not a hundred thousand politicians at the South, but a hundred thousand merchants and farmers here, who are more interested in commerce and agriculture than they are in humanity, and are not prepared to do justice to the slave and to Mexico, *cost what it may*. I quarrel not with far-off foes, but with those who, near at home, co-operate with, and do the bidding of those far away, and without whom the latter would be harmless. We are accustomed to say, that the mass of men are unprepared; but improvement is slow, because the few are not materially wiser or better than the many. It is not so important that many should be as good as you, as that there be some absolute goodness somewhere; for that will leaven the whole lump. There are thousands who are *in opinion* opposed to slavery and to the war, who yet in effect do nothing to put an end to them; who, esteeming themselves children of Washington and Franklin, sit down with their hands in their pockets, and say that they know not what to do, and do nothing; who even postpone the question of freedom to the question of free-trade, and quietly read the prices-current along with the latest advices from Mexico, after dinner, and, it may be, fall asleep over them both. What is the price-current of an honest man and patriot to-day? They hesitate, and they regret, and sometimes they petition; but they do nothing in earnest and with effect. They will wait, well disposed, for others to remedy the evil, that they may no longer have it to regret. At most, they give only a cheap vote, and a feeble countenance and Godspeed, to the right, as it goes by them. There are nine hundred and ninety-nine patrons of virtue to one virtuous man; but it is easier to deal with the real possessor of a thing than with the temporary guardian of it.

All voting is a sort of gaming, like chequers or backgammon, with a slight moral tinge to it, a playing with right and wrong, with moral questions; and betting naturally accompanies it. The character of the voters is not staked. I cast my vote, perchance, as I think right; but I am not vitally concerned that that right should prevail. I am willing to leave it to the majority. Its obligation, therefore, never exceeds that of expediency. Even voting *for the right* is *doing* nothing for it. It is only expressing to men feebly your desire that it should prevail. A wise man will not leave the right to the mercy of chance, nor wish it to prevail through the power of the majority. There is but little virtue in the action of masses of men. When the majority shall at length vote for the abolition of slavery, it will be because they are indifferent to slavery, or because there is but little slavery left to be abolished by their vote. *They* will then be the only slaves. Only *his* vote can hasten the abolition of slavery who asserts his own freedom by his vote.

I hear of a convention to be held at Baltimore, or elsewhere, for the selection of a candidate for the Presidency, made up chiefly of editors, and men who are politicians by profession; but I think, what is it to any independent, intelligent, and respectable man what decision they may come to, shall we not have the advantage of his wisdom and honesty, nevertheless? Can we not count upon some independent votes? Are there not many individuals in the country who do not attend conventions? But no: I find that the respectable man, so called, has immediately drifted from his position, and despairs of his country, when his country has more reason to despair of him. He forthwith adopts one of the candidates thus selected as the only *available* one, thus proving that he is himself *available* for any purposes of the demagogue. His vote is of no more worth than that of any unprincipled foreigner or hireling native, who may have been bought. Oh for a man who is a *man,* and, as my neighbor says, has a bone in his back which you cannot pass your hand through! Our statistics are at fault: the population has been returned too large. How many *men* are there to a square thousand miles in this country? Hardly one. Does not America offer any inducement for men to settle here? The American has dwindled into an Odd Fellow,—one who may be known by the development of his organ of gregariousness, and a manifest lack of intellect and cheerful self-reliance; whose first and chief concern, on coming into the world, is to see that the alms-houses are in good repair; and, before yet he has lawfully donned the virile garb, to collect a fund for the support of the widows and orphans that may be; who, in short, ventures to live only by the aid of the mutual insurance company, which has promised to bury him decently.

It is not a man's duty, as a matter of course, to devote himself to the eradication of any, even the most enormous wrong; he may still properly have other concerns to engage him; but it is his duty, at least, to wash his hands of it, and, if he gives it no thought longer, not to give it practically his support. If I devote myself to other pursuits and contemplations, I must first see, at least, that I do not pursue them sitting upon another man's shoulders. I must get off him first, that he may pursue his contemplations too. See what gross inconsistency is tolerated. I have heard some of my townsmen say, "I should like to have them order me out to help put down an insurrection of the slaves, or to march to Mexico,—see if I would go;" and yet these very men have each, directly by their allegiance, and so indirectly, at least, by their money, furnished a substitute. The soldier is applauded who refuses to serve in an unjust war by those who do not refuse to sustain the unjust government which makes the war; is applauded by those whose own act and authority he disregards and sets at nought; as if the State were penitent to that degree that it hired one to scourge it while it sinned, but not to that degree that it left off sinning for a moment. Thus, under the name of order and civil government, we are all made at last to pay homage to and support our own meanness. After the first blush of sin, comes its indifference; and from immoral it becomes, as it were, *un*moral, and not quite unnecessary to that life which we have made.

The broadest and most prevalent error requires the most disinterested virtue to sustain it. The slight reproach to which the virtue of patriotism is commonly liable, the noble are most likely to incur. Those who, while they disapprove of the character and measure of a government, yield to it their allegiance and support, are undoubtedly its most conscientious supporters, and so frequently the most serious obstacles to reform. Some are petitioning the State to dissolve the Union, to disregard the requisitions of the President. Why do they not dissolve it themselves,—the union between themselves and the State,—and refuse to pay their quota into its treasury? Do not they stand in the same relation to the State, that the State does to the Union? And have not the same reasons prevented the State from resisting the Union, which have prevented them from resisting the State?

How can a man be satisfied to entertain an opinion merely, and enjoy *it?* Is there any enjoyment in it, if his opinion is that he is aggrieved? If you are cheated out of a single dollar by your neighbor, you do not rest satisfied with knowing that you are cheated or with saying that you are cheated, or even with petitioning him to pay you your due; but you take effectual steps at once to obtain the full amount, and see that you are never cheated again. Action from principle,—the perception and the performance of right,—changes things and relations; it is essentially revolutionary, and does not consist wholly with any thing which was. It not only divides states and churches, it divides families, aye, it divides the *individual,* separating the diabolical in him from the divine.

Unjust laws exist; shall we be content to obey them, or shall we endeavor to amend them, and obey them until we have succeeded, or shall we transgress them at once? Men generally, under such a government as this, think that they ought to wait until they have persuaded the majority to alter them. They think that, if they should resist, the remedy would be worse than the evil. But it is the fault of the government itself that the remedy *is* worse than the evil. *It* makes it worse. Why is it not more apt to anticipate and provide for reform? Why does it not cherish its wise minority? Why does it cry and resist before it is hurt? Why does it not encourage its citizens to be on the alert to point out its faults, and *do* better than it would have them? Why does it always crucify Christ, and excommunicate Copernicus and Luther, and pronounce Washington and Franklin rebels?

One would think, that a deliberate and practical denial of its authority was the only offense never contemplated by government; else, why has it not assigned its definite, its suitable and proportionate penalty? If a man who has no property refuses but once to earn nine shillings for the State, he is put in prison for a period unlimited by any law that I know, and determined only by the discretion of those who placed him there; but if he should steal ninety times nine shillings from the State, he is soon permitted to go at large again.

If the injustice is part of the necessary friction of the machine of government, let it go, let it go; perchance it will wear smooth,—certainly the machine will wear out. If the injustice has a spring, or a pulley, or a rope, or a crank, exclusively for itself, then perhaps you may consider whether the remedy will not be worse than the evil; but if it is of such a nature that it requires you to be the agent of injustice to another, then, I say, break the law. Let your life be a counter friction to stop the machine. What I have to do is to see, at any rate, that I do not lend myself to the wrong which I condemn.

As for adopting the ways which the State has provided for remedying the evil, I know not of such ways. They take too much time, and a man's life will be gone. I have other affairs to attend to. I came into this world, not chiefly to make this a good place to live in, but to live in it, be it good or bad. A man has not every thing to do, but something; and because he cannot do *every thing*, it is not necessary that he should do *something* wrong. It is not my business to be petitioning the governor or the legislature any more than it is theirs to petition me; and, if they should not hear my petition, what should I do then? But in this case the State has provided no way: its very Constitution is the evil. This may seem to be harsh and stubborn and unconciliatory; but it is to treat with the utmost kindness and consideration the only spirit that can appreciate or deserve it. So is all change for the better, like birth and death which convulse the body.

I do not hesitate to say, that those who call themselves abolitionists should at once effectually withdraw their support, both in person and property, from the government of Massachusetts, and not wait till they constitute a majority of one, before they suffer the right to prevail through them. I think that it is enough if they have God on their side, without waiting for that other one. Moreover, any man more right than his neighbors constitutes a majority of one already.

I meet this American government, or its representative the State government, directly, and face to face, once a year, no more, in the person of its tax-gatherer; this is the only mode in which a man situated as I am necessarily meets it; and it then says distinctly, recognize me; and the simplest, the most effectual, and, in the present posture of affairs, the indispensablest mode of treating with it on this head, of expressing your little satisfaction with and love for it, is to deny it then. My civil neighbor, the tax-gatherer, is the very man I have to deal with,—for it is, after all, with men and not with parchment that I quarrel,—and he has voluntarily chosen to be an agent of the government. How shall he ever know well what he is and does as an officer of the government, or as a man, until he is obliged to consider whether he shall treat me, his neighbor, for whom he has respect, as a neighbor and well-disposed man, or as a maniac and disturber of the peace, and see if he can get over this obstruction to his neighborliness without a ruder and more impetuous thought or speech corresponding with his action? I know this well, that if one thousand, if one hundred, if ten men whom I could name,—if ten *honest* men only,—aye, if *one* HONEST man, in this State of Massachusetts, *ceasing to hold slaves,* were actually to withdraw from this copartnership, and be locked up in the county jail therefor, it would be the abolition of slavery in America. For it matters not how small the beginning may seem to be: what is once well done is done for ever. But we love better to talk about it: that we say is our mission. Reform keeps many scores of newspapers in its service, but not one man. If my esteemed neighbor, the State's ambassador, who will devote his days to the settlement of the question of human rights in the Council Chamber, instead of being threatened with the prisons of Carolina, were to sit down the prisoner of Massachusetts, that State which is so anxious to foist the sin of slavery upon her sister,—though at present she can discover only an act of inhospitality to be the ground of a quarrel with her,—the Legislature would not wholly waive the subject the following winter.

Under a government which imprisons any unjustly, the true place for a just man is also a prison. The proper place to-day, the only place which Massachusetts has provided for her freer and less desponding spirits, is in her prisons, to be put out and locked out of the State by her own act, as they have already put themselves out by their principles. It is there that the fugitive slave, and the Mexican prisoner on parole, and the Indian come to plead the wrongs of his race, should find them; on that separate, but more free and honorable ground, where the State places those who are not *with* her but *against* her,—the only house in a slave-state in which a free man can abide with honor. If any think that their influence would be lost there, and their voices no longer afflict the ear of the State, that they would not be as an enemy within its walls, they do not know by how much truth is stronger than error, nor how much more eloquently and effectively he can combat injustice who has experienced a little in his own person. Cast your whole vote, not a strip of paper merely, but your whole influence. A minority is powerless while it conforms to the majority; it is not even a minority then; but it is irresistible when it clogs by its whole weight. If the alternative is to keep all just men in prison, or give up war and slavery, the State will not hesitate which to choose. If a thousand men were not to pay their tax-bills this year, that would not be a violent and bloody measure, as it would be to pay them, and enable the State to commit violence and shed innocent blood. This is, in fact, the definition of a peaceful revolution, if any such is possible. If the tax-gatherer, or any other public officer, asks me, as one has done, "But what shall I do?" my answer is, "If you really wish to do any thing, resign your office." When the subject has refused allegiance, and the officer has resigned his office, then the revolution is accomplished. But even suppose blood should flow. Is there not a sort of blood shed when the conscience is wounded? Through this wound a man's real manhood and immortality flow out, and he bleeds to an everlasting death. I see this blood flowing now.

I have contemplated the imprisonment of the offender, rather than the seizure of his goods,—though both will serve the same purpose,—because they who assert the purest right, and consequently are most dangerous to a corrupt State, commonly have not spent much time in accumulating property. To such the State renders comparatively small service, and a slight tax is wont to appear exorbitant, particularly if they are obliged to earn it by special labor with their hands. If there were one who lived wholly without the use of money, the State itself would hesitate to demand it of him. But the rich man—not to make any invidious comparison—is always sold to the institution which makes him rich. Absolutely speaking, the more money, the less virtue; for money comes between a man and his objects, and obtains them for him; and it was certainly no great virtue to obtain it. It puts to rest many questions which he would otherwise be taxed to answer; while the only new question which it puts is the hard but superfluous one, how to spend it. Thus his moral ground is taken from under his feet. The opportunities of living are diminished in proportion as what are called the "means" are increased. The best thing a man can do for his culture when he is rich is to endeavor to carry out those schemes which he entertained when he was poor. Christ answered the Herodians according to their condition. "Show me the tribute-money," said he;—and one took a penny out of his pocket;—if you use money which has the image of Caesar on it, and which he has made current and valuable, that is, *if you are men of the State,* and gladly enjoy the advantages of Caesar's government, then pay him back some of his own when he demands it; "Render therefore to Caesar that which is Caesar's, and to God those things which are God's,"—leaving them no wiser than before as to which was which; for they did not wish to know.

When I converse with the freest of my neighbors, I perceive that, whatever they may say about the magnitude and seriousness of the question, and their regard for the public tranquillity, the long and the short of the matter is, that they cannot spare the protection of the existing government, and they dread the consequences of disobedience to it to their property and families. For my own part, I should not like to think that I ever rely on the protection of the State. But, if I deny the authority of the State when it presents its tax-bill, it will soon take and waste all my property, and so harass me and my children without end. This is hard. This makes it impossible for a man to live honestly and at the same time comfortably in outward respects. It will not be worth the while to accumulate property; that would be sure to go again. You must hire or squat somewhere, and raise but a small crop, and eat that soon. You must live within yourself, and depend upon yourself, always tucked up and ready for a start, and not have many affairs. A man may grow rich in Turkey even, if he will be in all respects a good subject of the Turkish government. Confucius said,—"If a State is governed by the principles of reason, poverty and misery are subjects of shame; if a State is not governed by the principles of reason, riches and honors are the subjects of shame." No: until I want the protection of Massachusetts to be extended to me in some distant southern port, where my liberty is endangered, or until I am bent solely on building up an estate at home by peaceful enterprise, I can afford to refuse allegiance to Massachusetts, and her right to my property and life. It costs me less in every sense to incur the penalty of disobedience to the State, than it would to obey. I should feel as if I were worth less in that case.

Some years ago, the State met me in behalf of the church, and commanded me to pay a certain sum toward the support of a clergyman whose preaching my father attended, but never I myself. "Pay it," it said, "or be locked up in the jail." I declined to pay. But, unfortunately another man saw fit to pay it. I did not see why the schoolmaster should be taxed to support the priest, and not the priest the schoolmaster: for I was not the State's schoolteacher, but I supported myself by voluntary subscription. I did not see why the lyceum should not present its tax-bill, and have the State to back its demand, as well as the church. However, at the request of the selectmen, I condescended to make some such statement as this in writing:—"Know all men by these presents, that I, Henry Thoreau, do not wish to be regarded as a member of any incorporated society which I have not joined." This I gave to the town-clerk; and he has it. The State, having thus learned that I did not wish to be regarded as a member of that church, has never made a like demand on me since; though it said that it must adhere to its original presumption that time. If I had known how to name them, I should then have signed off in detail from all the societies which I never signed on to; but I did not know where to find a complete list.

I have paid no poll-tax for six years. I was put into a jail once on this account, for one night; and, as I stood considering the walls of solid stone, two or three feet thick, the door of wood and iron, a foot thick, and the iron grating which strained the light, I could not help being struck with the foolishness of that institution which treated me as if I were mere flesh and blood and bones, to be locked up. I wondered that it should have concluded at length that this was the best use it could put me to, and had never thought to avail itself of my services in some way. I saw that, if there was a wall of stone between me and my townsmen, there was a still more difficult one to climb or break through, before they could get to be as free as I was. I did not for a moment feel confined, and the walls seemed a great waste of stone and mortar. I felt as if I alone of all my townsmen had paid my tax. They plainly did not know how to treat me, but behaved like persons who are under-bred. In every threat and in every compliment there was a blunder; for they thought that my chief desire was to stand the other side of that stone wall. I could not but smile to see how industriously they locked the door on my meditations, which followed them out again without let or hindrance, and *they* were really all that was dangerous. As they could not reach me, they had resolved to punish my body; just as boys, if they cannot come at some person against whom they have a spite, will abuse his dog. I saw that the State was half-witted, that it was timid as a lone woman with her silver spoons, and that it did not know its friends from its foes, and I lost all my remaining respect for it, and pitied it.

Thus the State never intentionally confronts a man's sense, intellectual or moral, but only his body, his senses. It is not armed with superior wit or honesty, but with superior physical strength. I was not born to be forced. I will breathe after my own fashion. Let us see who is the strongest. What force has a multitude? They only can force me who obey a higher law than I. They force me to become like themselves. I do not hear of *men* being *forced* to live this way or that by masses of men. What sort of life were that to live? When I meet a government which says to me, "Your money or your life," why should I be in haste to give it my money? It may be in a great strait, and not know what to do: I cannot help that. It must help itself: do as I do. It is not worth the while to snivel about. I am not responsible for the successful working of the machinery of society. I am not the son of the engineer. I perceive that, when an acorn and a chestnut fall side by side, the one does not remain inert to make way for the other, but both obey their own laws, and spring and grow and flourish as best they can, till one, perchance, overshadows and destroys the other. If a plant cannot live according to its nature, it dies; and so a man.

The night in prison was novel and interesting enough. The prisoners in their shirt-sleeves were enjoying a chat and the evening air in the door-way, when I entered. But the jailer said, "Come, boys, it is time to lock up;" and so they dispersed, and I heard the sound of their steps returning into the hollow apartments. My roommate was introduced to me by the jailer, as "a first-rate fellow and a clever man." When the door was locked, he showed me where to hang my hat, and how he managed matters there. The rooms were white-washed once a month; and this one, at least, was the whitest, most simply furnished, and probably the neatest apartment in the town. He naturally wanted to know where I came from, and what brought me there; and, when I had told him, I asked him in turn how he came there, presuming him to be an honest man, of course; and, as the world goes, I believe he was. "Why," said he, "they accuse me of burning a barn; but I never did it." As near as I could discover, he had probably gone to bed in a barn when drunk, and smoked his pipe there; and so a barn was burnt. He had the reputation of being a clever man, had been there some three months waiting for his trial to come on, and would have to wait as much longer; but he was quite domesticated and contented, since he got his board for nothing, and thought that he was well treated.

He occupied one window, and I the other; and I saw, that, if one stayed there long, his principal business would be to look out the window. I had soon read all the tracts that were left there, and examined where former prisoners had broken out, and where a grate had been sawed off, and heard the history of the various occupants of that room; for I found that even here there was a history and a gossip which never circulated beyond the walls of the jail. Probably this is the only house in the town where verses are composed, which are afterward printed in circular form, but not published. I was shown quite a long list of verses which were composed by some young men who had been detected in an attempt to escape, who avenged themselves by singing them.

I pumped my fellow-prisoner as dry as I could, for fear I should never see him again; but at length he showed me which was my bed, and left me to blow out the lamp.

It was like travelling into a far country, such as I had never expected to behold, to lie there for one night. It seemed to me that I never had heard the town-clock strike before, nor the evening sounds of the village; for we slept with the windows open, which were inside the grating. It was to see my native village in the light of the middle ages, and our Concord was turned into a Rhine stream, and visions of knights and castles passed before me. They were the voices of old burghers that I heard in the streets. I was an involuntary spectator and auditor for whatever was done and said in the kitchen of the adjacent village-inn,—a wholly new and rare experience to me. It was a closer view of my native town. I was fairly inside of it. I never had seen its institutions before. This is one of its peculiar institutions; for it is a shire town. I began to comprehend what its inhabitants were about.

In the morning, our breakfasts were put through the hole in the door, in small oblong-square tin pans, made to fit, and holding a pint of chocolate, with brown bread, and an iron spoon. When they called for the vessels again, I was green enough to return what bread I had left; but my comrade seized it, and said that I should lay that up for lunch or dinner. Soon after, he was let out to work at haying in a neighboring field, whither he went every day, and would not be back till noon; so he bade me good-day, saying that he doubted if he should see me again.

When I came out of prison,—for some one interfered, and paid the tax,—I did not perceive that great changes had taken place on the common, such as he observed who went in a youth, and emerged a tottering and gray-headed man; and yet a change had to my eyes come over the scene,—the town, and State, and country,—greater than any that mere time could effect. I saw to what extent the people among whom I lived could be trusted as good neighbors and friends;

119

that their friendship was for summer weather only; that they did not greatly purpose to do right; that they were a distinct race from me by their prejudices and superstitions, as the Chinamen and Malays are; that, in their sacrifices to humanity, they ran no risks, not even to their property; that, after all, they were not so noble but they treated the thief as he had treated them, and hoped, by a certain outward observance and a few prayers, and by walking in a particular straight though useless path from time to time, to save their souls. This may be to judge my neighbors harshly; for I believe that most of them are not aware that they have such an institution as the jail in their village.

It was formerly the custom in our village, when a poor debtor came out of jail, for his acquaintances to salute him, looking through their fingers, which were crossed to represent the grating of a jail window, "How do ye do?" My neighbors did not thus salute me, but first looked at me, and then at one another, as if I had returned from a long journey. I was put into jail as I was going to the shoemaker's to get a shoe which was mended. When I was let out the next morning, I proceeded to finish my errand, and, having put on my mended shoe, joined a huckleberry party, who were impatient to put themselves under my conduct; and in half an hour,—for the horse was soon tackled,—was in the midst of a huckleberry field, on one of our highest hills, two miles off; and then the State was nowhere to be seen.

This is the whole history of "My Prisons."

I have never declined paying the highway tax, because I am as desirous of being a good neighbor as I am of being a bad subject; and, as for supporting schools, I am doing my part to educate my fellow-countrymen now. It is for no particular item in the tax-bill that I refuse to pay it. I simply wish to refuse allegiance to the State, to withdraw and stand aloof from it effectually. I do not care to trace the course of my dollar, if I could, till it buys a man, or a musket to shoot one with,—the dollar is innocent,—but I am concerned to trace the effects of my allegiance. In fact, I quietly declare war with the State, after my fashion, though I will still make what use and get what advantage of her I can, as is usual in such cases.

If others pay the tax which is demanded of me, from a sympathy with the State, they do but what they have already done in their own case, or rather they abet injustice to a greater extent than the State requires. If they pay a tax from a mistaken interest in the individual taxed, to save his going to jail, it is because they have not considered wisely how far they let their private feelings interfere with the public good.

This, then, is my position at present. But one cannot be too much on his guard in such a case, lest his action be biased by obstinacy, or an undue regard for the opinions of men. Let him see that he does only what belongs to himself and to the hour.

I think sometimes, Why, this people mean well; they are only ignorant; they would do better if they knew how; why give your neighbors this pain to treat you as they are not inclined to? But I think, again, this is no reason why I should do as they do, or permit others to suffer much greater pain of a different kind. Again, I sometimes say to myself, when many millions of men, without heat, without ill-will, without personal feeling of any kind, demand of you a few shillings only, without the possibility, such is their constitution, of retracting or altering their present demand, and without the possibility, on your side, of appeal to any other millions, why expose yourself to this overwhelming brute force? You do not resist cold and hunger, the winds and the waves, thus obstinately; you quietly submit to a thousand similar necessities. You do not put your head into the fire. But just in proportion as I regard this as not wholly a brute force, but partly a human force, and consider that I have relations to those millions as to so many millions of men, and not of mere brute or inanimate things, I see that appeal is possible, first and instantaneously, from them to the Maker of them, and, secondly, from them to themselves. But, if I put my head deliberately into the fire, there is no appeal to fire or to the Maker of fire, and I have only myself to blame. If I could convince myself that I have any right to be satisfied with men as they are, and to treat them accordingly, and not according, in some respects, to my requisitions and expectations of what they and I ought to be, then, like a good Mussulman and fatalist, I should endeavor to be satisfied with things as they are, and say it is the will of God. And, above all, there is this difference between resisting this and a purely brute or natural force, that I can resist this with some effect; but I cannot expect, like Orpheus, to change the nature of the rocks and trees and beasts.

I do not wish to quarrel with any man or nation. I do not wish to split hairs, to make fine distinctions, or set myself up as better than my neighbors. I seek rather, I may say, even an excuse for conforming to the laws of the land. I am but too ready to conform to them. Indeed I have reason to suspect myself on this head; and each year, as the tax-gatherer comes around, I find myself disposed to review the acts and position of the general and state governments, and the spirit of the people, to discover a pretext for conformity. I believe that the State will soon be able to take all my work of this sort out of my hands, and then I shall be no better a patriot than my fellow-country-men. Seen from a lower point of view, the Constitution, with all its faults, is very good; the law and the courts are very respectable; even this State and this American government are, in many respects, very admirable and rare things, to be thankful for, such as a great many have described them; but seen from a point of view a little higher, they are what I have described them; seen from a higher still, and the highest, who shall say what they are, or that they are worth looking at or thinking of at all?

However, the government does not concern me much, and I shall bestow the fewest possible thoughts on it. It is not many moments that I live under a government, even in this world. If a man is thought-free, fancy-free, imagination-free, that which *is not* never for a long time appearing *to be* to him, unwise rulers or reformers cannot fatally interrupt him.

I know that most men think differently from myself; but those whose lives are by profession devoted to the study of these or kindred subjects, content me as little as any. Statesmen and legislators, standing so completely within the institution, never distinctly and nakedly behold it. They speak of moving society, but have no resting-place without it. They may be men of a certain experience and discrimination, and have no doubt invented ingenious and even useful systems, for which we sincerely thank them; but all their wit and usefulness lie within certain not very wide limits. They are wont to forget that the world is not governed by policy and expediency. Webster never goes behind government, and so cannot speak with authority about it. His words are wisdom to those legislators who contemplate no essential reform in the existing government; but for thinkers, and those who legislate for all time, he never once glances at the subject. I know of those whose serene and wise speculations on this theme would soon reveal the limits of his mind's range and hospitality. Yet, compared with the cheap professions of most reformers, and the still cheaper wisdom and eloquence of politicians in general, his are almost the only sensible and valuable words, and we thank Heaven for him. Comparatively, he is always strong, original, and, above all, practical. Still his quality is not wisdom, but prudence. The lawyer's truth is not truth, but consistency, or a consistent expediency. Truth is always in harmony with herself, and is not concerned chiefly to reveal the justice that may consist with wrong-doing. He well deserves to be called, as he has been called, the Defender of the Constitution. There are really no blows to be given by him but defensive ones. He is not a leader, but a follower. His leaders are the men of '87. "I have never made an effort," he says, "and never propose to make an effort; I have never countenanced an effort, and never mean to countenance an effort, to disturb the arrangement as originally made, by which the various States came into the Union." Still thinking of the sanction which the Constitution gives to slavery, he says, "Because it was a part of the original compact,—let it stand." Notwithstanding his special acuteness and ability, he is unable to take a fact out of its merely political relations, and behold it as it lies absolutely to be disposed of by the intellect,—what, for instance, it behoves a man to do here in America to-day with regard to slavery, but ventures, or is driven, to make some such desperate answer as the following, while professing to speak absolutely, and as a private man,—from which what new and singular code of social duties might be inferred?—"The manner," says he, "in which the governments of those States where slavery exists are to regulate it, is for their own consideration, under their responsibility to their constituents, to the general laws of propriety, humanity, and justice, and to God. Associations formed elsewhere, springing from a feeling of humanity, or any other cause, have nothing what-

ever to do with it. They have never received any encourage-
ment from me, and they never will."

They who know of no purer sources of truth, who have
traced up its stream no higher, stand, and wisely stand, by
the Bible and the Constitution, and drink at it there with
reverence and humility; but they who behold where it comes
trickling into this lake or that pool, gird up their loins once
more, and continue their pilgrimage toward its fountain-
head.

No man with a genius for legislation has appeared in America. They are rare in the history of the world. There are ora-
tors, politicians, and eloquent men, by the thousand; but the
speaker has not yet opened his mouth to speak, who is capable of settling the much-vexed questions of the day. We love
eloquence for its own sake, and not for any truth which it
may utter, or any heroism it may inspire. Our legislators
have not yet learned the comparative value of free-trade and
of freedom, of union, and of rectitude, to a nation. They have
no genius or talent for comparatively humble questions of
taxation and finance, commerce and manufactures and agriculture. If we were left solely to the wordy wit of legislators
in Congress for our guidance, uncorrected by the seasonable
experience and the effectual complaints of the people, America would not long retain her rank among the nations. For
eighteen hundred years, though perchance I have no right
to say it, the New Testament has been written; yet where is
the legislator who has wisdom and practical talent enough
to avail himself of the light which it sheds on the science of
legislation?

The authority of government, even such as I am willing to
submit to,—for I will cheerfully obey those who know and
can do better than I, and in many things even those who
neither know nor can do so well,—is still an impure one: to
be strictly just, it must have the sanction and consent of the
governed. It can have no pure right over my person and
property but what I concede to it. The progress from an absolute to a limited monarchy, from a limited monarchy to a
democracy, is a progress toward a true respect for the individual. Is a democracy, such as we know it, the last improvement possible in government? Is it not possible to take

a step further towards recognizing and organizing the rights of man? There will never be a really free and enlightened State, until the State comes to recognize the individual as a higher and independent power, from which all its own power and authority are derived, and treats him accordingly. I please myself with imagining a State at last which can afford to be just to all men, and to treat the individual with respect as a neighbor; which even would not think it inconsistent with its own repose, if a few were to live aloof from it, not meddling with it, nor embraced by it, who fulfilled all the duties of neighbors and fellow-men. A State which bore this kind of fruit, and suffered it to drop off as fast as it ripened, would prepare the way for a still more perfect and glorious State, which also I have imagined, but not yet anywhere seen.

Factors of mature style

Average number of words per sentence

AMOUNT USED AS SAMPLE

(specific amount—words, sentences, pages, or chapters)
105 sentences; approximately 28 percent of the total work

LOCATION OF THE SAMPLE

(beginning, middle, end; or any two or all three)
first 105 sentences

AVERAGE

24.7 words per sentence

COMMENTARY

This average exceeds the average for professionals as suggested in Chapter One. This suggests that Thoreau's style has a heavy, unreadable' quality about it. Philosophical dissertations tend to be wordy and complex, but Thoreau uses many short sentences, especially in the form of rhetorical questions, to lighten the overall effect.

Variation in sentence length

AMOUNT USED AS SAMPLE

(specific amount—words, sentences, pages, or chapters)
105 sentences; approximately 28 percent of the total work

LOCATION OF THE SAMPLE

(beginning, middle, end; or any two or all three)
first 105 sentences

VARIATION

shortest sentence—2 words
longest sentence—97 words

COMMENTARY

The statistic above indicates Thoreau writes both the short
sentence and the long sentence. A reading of his essay reveals
that both short and long sentences read well, the long ones cap-
ably constructed to carry complex ideas.

Frequency of free modifiers

AMOUNT USED AS SAMPLE

(specific amount—words, sentences, pages, or chapters)
105 sentences; approximately 28 percent of the total work

LOCATION OF THE SAMPLE

(beginning, middle, end; or any two or all three)
first 105 sentences

FREQUENCY

922 free modifiers or 34 percent of the total
569 or 61 percent in the final position

COMMENTARY

Thoreau's writing easily fits the criterion, a high frequency of
free modifiers, especially in the final position. He uses a variety
of free modifiers or syntactic structures with a special fondness
for dependent clauses.

Frequency of intra-T-unit coordination

AMOUNT USED AS SAMPLE

(specific amount—words, sentences, pages, or chapters)
105 sentences; approximately 28 percent of the total work

LOCATION OF THE SAMPLE

(beginning, middle, end; or any two or all three)
first 105 sentences

FREQUENCY

129 T-units, 51 with some intra-T-unit coordination; 39 percent with coordination

COMMENTARY

Although Thoreau does not use intra-T-unit coordination with as high a frequency as those writers discussed in Chapter One, he does, nevertheless, use a respectable amount of coordination.

Syntactic structures

Appositive

Visit the Navy Yard, and behold a marine, such a man as an American government can make, or such as it can make a man with its black arts, a mere shadow and reminiscence of humanity, a man laid out alive and standing, and already, as one may say, buried under arms with funeral accompaniments. . . .

Participle

In the morning, our breakfasts were put through the hole in the door, in small oblong-square tin pans, made to fit, and holding a pint of chocolate, with brown bread, and an iron spoon.

Gerund

Even voting *for the right* is *doing* nothing for it.

Infinitive

I simply wish to refuse allegiance to the State, to withdraw and stand aloof from it effectually.

Parallel construction

It not only divides States and churches, it divides families; aye, it divides the *individual,* separating the diabolical in him from the divine.

Absolute

But Paley appears never to have contemplated those cases to which the rule of expediency does not apply, in which a people, as well as an individual, must do justice, cost what it may.

Adjective clause

He who gives himself entirely to his fellow-men appears to them useless and selfish; but he who gives himself partially to them is pronounced a benefactor and philanthropist.

Adverb clause

No: until I want the protection of Massachusetts to be extended to me in some distant Southern part, where my liberty is endangered, or until I am bent solely on building up an estate at home by peaceful enterprise, I can afford to refuse allegiance to Massachusetts, and her right to my property and life.

Noun clause

What I have to do is to see, at any rate, that I do not lend myself to the wrong which I condemn.

Rhetoric of productive sentences

Multi-level sentence (at least four levels)

EXAMPLE

A common and natural result of an undue respect for law is, that you may see a file of soldiers, colonel, captain, corporal, privates, powder-monkeys, and all, marching in admirable order over hill and dale to the wars, against their wills, aye, against their common sense and consciences, which makes it very steep marching indeed, and produces a palpitation of the heart.

DIAGRAMMED

1 A common and natural result of an undue respect for law is, that you may see a file of soldiers,
  2 colonel, captain, corporal, privates, powder-monkeys, and all,
  2 marching in admirable order over hill and dale to the wars,
    3 against their wills,
    3 aye, against their common sense and consciences,
      4 which makes it very steep marching indeed, and produces a palpitation of the heart.

COMMENTARY

Apparently, Thoreau's use of the comma differs from contemporary usage. Note the comma following the verb "is" in the independent clause, or level one. Assuming this difference, one can see that the noun clause after the linking verb functions as a predicate noun. Thoreau follows this with an appositive phrase enumerating the soldiers and with a participial phrase describing them. At level three he constructs two parallel prepositional phrases, both using the word "against." For the final level, level four, he employs a dependent adjective clause containing a compound verb.

Verb density

AMOUNT USED AS SAMPLE

(specific amount—words, sentences, pages, or chapters)

105 sentences; approximately 28 percent of the total work

(beginning, middle, end; or any two or all three)
first 105 sentences

DENSITY
(1:5 to 1:8 represents the acceptable ratio)
$385:2599 = 1:7$

COMMENTARY

The ratio of verbs and verbals to the total number of words lies well within the ideal range. This indicates Thoreau is not guilty of writing a heavy, verbless prose. In fact, he writes a richly textured, vivid style that ably conveys complex ideas with clarity.

Rhetoric of productive paragraphs

Multi-level paragraph (at least four levels)

EXAMPLE

Unjust laws exist: shall we be content to obey them, or shall we endeavor to amend them, and obey them until we have succeeded, or shall we transgress them at once? Men generally, under such a government as this, think that they ought to wait until they have persuaded the majority to alter them. They think that, if they should resist, the remedy would be worse than the evil. But it is the fault of the government itself that the remedy *is* worse than the evil. *It* makes it worse. Why is it not more apt to anticipate and provide for reform? Why does it not cherish its wise minority? Why does it cry and resist before it is hurt? Why does it not encourage its citizens to be on the alert to point out its faults, and *do* better than it would have them? Why does it always crucify Christ, and excommunicate Copernicus and Luther, and pronounce Washington and Franklin rebels?

1 Unjust laws . . . at once?
  2 Men generally . . . alter them.
  2 They think . . . the evil.
    3 But it . . . the evil.
      4 *It* makes it worse.
      4 Why is . . . for reform?
      4 Why does . . . wise minority?
      4 Why does . . . is hurt?
      4 Why does . . . have them?
      4 Why does . . . Franklin rebels?

COMMENTARY

Having offered three possible courses of action in his top sentence (level one), Thoreau proceeds to comment on the second and third possibilities in a pair of level two sentences. The latter of these two sentences provides a phrase that leads him to his level three, where he blames the government. The remainder of the paragraph, six level four sentences, comments on the government by using the pronoun "it" and a series of five rhetorical questions. Such rhetorical questions, questions designed for effect and emphasis, but not requiring an answer, appear frequently in Thoreau, who uses them with great skill. Using these structures results in a tightly written paragraph, employing parallelism to carry his attack on the government and to emphasize his feelings.

Semantic structures

Simile

I saw that the State was half-witted, that it was timid as a lone woman with her silver spoons, and that it did not know its friends from its foes, and I lost all remaining respect for it, and pitied it.

Metaphor

It [the American government] is a sort of wooden gun to the people themselves.

Appendix A

List of euphemisms

I am reminded of the man who filled in an application for an insurance policy. One of the questions he had to answer was 'How old was your father when he died and of what did he die?' Well, his father had been hanged, but he did not like to put that in his application. He puzzled over it for quite a while. He finally wrote, 'My father was sixty-five when he died. He came to his end while participating in a public function when the platform gave way.'

—Senator Everett Dirksen, in the Senate

adultery: infidelity
ambulance: invalid-coach

bad breath: halitosis
bankruptcy: straitened financial
  circumstances
bar: cocktail lounge
    tavern
barber: chirotonsor
    tonsorial artist
bedding manufacturer:
  mattress-engineer
  sleep engineer
blind: visually handicapped
boarder: paying guest
bookkeeper: accountant

breast of chicken: white meat
bury (the dead): enshrine
             entomb
             immure
             inter
             lay to rest
bus boy: table service man
butcher: meattrimmer

cemetery: *see* graveyard
cheat: depend on others to
  do his work
cleaning woman: cleaning lady
clerk: salesperson
coffin: casket

concentration camp:
 relocation center
corpse: dear departed
  mortal remains
  the deceased
  the loved one
crazy: mentally ill
crime: transgression

damn: dang
 darn
 dash
dead: cold
  deceased
  no longer with us
  gone from us
  gone to his reward
death: your loss
  his passing
die: to depart this world
 to expire
 to go from us
 to leave this vale of tears
 to pass away
 to pass on
 to go to his rest
dishwasher:
 utensil maintenance man
disorganized retreat:
 planned withdrawal
dole: public assistance
door-to-door salesman:
 customer contact personnel
drink: imbibe
 quaff
drunk: inebriated
 intoxicated
 three sheets to the wind
 feeling no pain
drunkenness: intemperance
  overindulgence

eat: partake of
electrician: electrical contractor

failed: almost passed
fake: artificial
false teeth: dentures
fat: portly
 stout
file clerk: research consultant
fire him:
 terminate his employment
 ask for his resignation
floorwalker: aisle manager
foot-doctor: chiropodist
  podiatrist
forcible expatriation:
 resettlement
foreman: plant superintendent
  supervisory personnel
fortunetellers: clairvoyants
  readers
funeral: obsequies

garage: lubritorium
garbage collector:
 sanitary engineer
garbage men:
 see garbage collector
garbage truck: sanitation vehicle
gardener: landscape architect
gas station attendant:
 serviceman
glutton: gourmand
  trencherman
gluttony: overindulgence
God: gad
 golly
 gosh
graveyard: cemetery
  memorial garden
  memorial park
grease job: lubrication service
grease pit: see garage

hairdresser: beautician
  beauty consultant

head accountant: vice-president
  in charge of finance
head truant officer: director of
  pupil personnel
head waiter: maître d'hôtel
hearse: limousine
hell: heck
hired girls: domestics
hired men: dairy assistants
house trailer: mobile home
house wrecker:
  demolition engineer

insane: emotionally disturbed
  mentally ill
insane asylum: state hospital
  sanitarium
  rest home
installment buying:
  deferred payment
  installment plan
insurance salesman:
  field underwriter

jail: reformatory
  penitentiary
  detention center
janitor: custodian
job: position
juke box:
  automatic coin machine
junior box-office clerk:
  assistant treasurer

kitchen:
  food preparation laboratory

ladies' underwear:
  lingerie
  unmentionables
lie down: go to bed
laying off: *see* fire him
lazy: indolent
  unmotivated

legs: limbs
  lower extremities
lie: fib
  misrepresentation
  story
  tendency to stretch the truth
  white lie
liquor store: spirit shop
  wine emporium
  package store
  state store
  green front
lodger: *see* boarder

maid: housekeeper
manure: plant food
  fertilizer
milkman: route salesman
mortuary: slumber room

office girl: receptionist
  secretary
old people: senior citizens
  the elderly
  golden-agers

pawnbrokers:
  proprietors of loan offices
plumber: sanitary engineer
poor: financially embarrassed
  low income group
  underprivileged
poorhouse: county home
  nursing home
poverty-stricken:
  disadvantaged
  underprivileged
pregnant: enceinte
  gravid
  to be expecting
  to be in a family way
press agent:
  contact manager
  publicist
  public relations counselor

publicity agent:
    public relations advisor
pull teeth: extract teeth
            perform extractions

raised: revised upward
rat-catcher:
    exterminating engineer
    extermination engineer
    exterminator
real estate agent: realtor
retreat: defensive maneuver
        retrograde action
        redeployment
        reform positions

salesman:
    company representative
    customer's representative
    sales engineer
    sales representative
saloon: *see* bar
selling: merchandising
shell shock: battle fatigue
shoemaker: cobblers
            shoe-rebuilders
shoplifting, losses from:
    inventory shrinkage
shroud: negligee
        slumber shirt
        slumber robe
sick: ill
    indisposed
slum clearance: urban renewal
slums:
    older, more overcrowded
        areas
    culturally deprived areas
spade: engineering tool
spinster: bachelor girl
        career girl
spit: expectorate

steal: take without permission
        appropriate
        make a midnight
            requisition
steerage: tourist class
stupid: retarded
        slow
sweat: perspire
        glow

tailor: stylist
tax collector:
    internal revenue agent
toilet: bathroom
        ladies' room
        men's room
        powder room
        rest room
toothpaste: dentifrice
tramp: homeless unemployed
trash collector: *see* garbage
        collector
traveling salesman:
    field representative
tree-pruners: tree surgeons

undertaker: funeral director
            memorial counselor
            mortician
uneducated people:
    culturally deprived

waitresses: hostesses
went to bed: retired
wiretapping:
    invasion of privacy
        (against you)
    protective monitoring
        (against someone else)
without money:
    financially embarrassed
    without funds

Appendix B

List of clichés

A bird in the hand is worth two in the bush.
above-mentioned
abreast of the times
abysmal ignorance
Accidents will happen.
according to a usually reliable source
according to Hoyle
according to Webster
ace in the hole
ace up one's sleeve
achieve a radical transformation
Achilles' heel
aching void
acid test
add insult to injury
a factor in the problem
after all is said and done
against the elements
A little learning is a dangerous thing.
All good things must come to an end.
all nature seemed to
all of the people
All's well that ends well.

All that glitters is not gold.
all the luck in the world
All the world's a stage.
all things considered
all things to all men
all to the good
all work and no play
almighty dollar
alongside of
along this line; along these lines; along the lines of
amass a fortune
a matter of life or death
an axe to grind
ants in your pants
apple of his eye
are in receipt of
armed to the teeth
as luck would have it
as much fun as a barrel of monkeys
assembled multitude
as the crow flies
at a loss for words
at an early date
at a snail's pace
at one fell swoop

at your earliest convenience
autumn of his years
avoid like the plague

bad apple
bag and baggage
balmy breezes
battle royal
battle to a scoreless tie
be able to shrug off
beard the lion
bear in mind
beastial atrocities
beat a hasty retreat
beat around the bush
beaten track
beautiful but dumb
Beauty is only skin deep.
bed of roses
before the dawn of civilization
beggars description
beg the question
belabor the point
believe it or not
bend every effort
benefit of the doubt
best foot forward
best laid plans of mice and men
be that as it may
be there with bells on
better half
better late than never
beyond the shadow of a doubt
bid farewell
big as a house
big as life
big city
bigger and better
birds and bees
birds of a feather
bitter end
black as a crow
black as coal
black as ink
black as pitch

blank despair
blanket of snow
blessing in disguise
blew my top
blind as a bat
blind leading the blind
blissfully happy
blissfully ignorant
bloodstained tyranny
blue as the sky
blunt instrument
blushing bride
boast a finer collection
bolt out of the blue; bolt from
   the blue
bone of contention
bones to pick
boundless blue sky
bows in defeat
brave as a lion
brave the elements
break it to them gently
breakneck speed
break the ice
breathless silence
bright as a button
bring order out of chaos
bring the matter up
briny deep
broad daylight
brown as a berry
brown as a nut
buck up
budding genius
bull in the china shop
burning my candle at both ends
burning question; burning issue
burn the midnight oil
bury my nose in a book
bury the hatchet
bustling metropolis
busy as a beaver
busy as a bee; a busy bee; busy
   as bees
by and large

by leaps and bounds
by the same token

call a halt to
calm before the storm
cannot make head or tail of
can't hold a candle to it
captain of industry
cares weigh heavily
cart before the horse
carte blanche
carry coals to Newcastle
caught between the devil and
  the deep blue sea
caught like a rat in a trap
center of attraction
chalk up a victory
champing at the bit
checkered career
cheeks like roses; rosy cheeks
chicken feed
chip off the old block
clammy hands
clean as a whistle
clean break
clear as a bell
clear as crystal; crystal clear
clinging vine
clockwork precision
cloud nine
clumsy as an ox
coin phrases
cold as a statue
cold as ice
cold blood
cold, hard cash
cold shoulder
come through with flying colors
come to the rescue
common as dirt
commune with nature
comparisons are odious
conspicuous by its absence
constructive criticism
consumed by flames

consummation devoutly to be
  wished
cool as a cucumber
cooling western breeze
coos like a dove
couldn't hit the broad side of a
  barn
countless generations
covered like a blanket
covers a multitude of sins
crack of dawn
crack of doom
cradle of the deep
crazy like a fox
credibility gap
Crime doesn't pay.
crocodile tears
cross as a bear
crowned with success
crowning glory
crushing blow
crushing defeat
crying shame
cry like a baby
cry wolf
cut-and-dried issue

darkness overtook him
dawn breaks
day after day
days on end
deader than a doornail; dead as
  a doornail
deadly earnest
dead of night
deaf as a post
dedicate ourselves anew
deem it a privilege; deem it an
  honor and a privilege
deepest gratitude
deliberate falsehood
demon rum
depths of despair
diabolical skill
diamond-in-the-rough

dire necessity
dirt cheap
disaster overtakes them
discreet silence
doesn't eat enough to keep a
 bird alive
dog's life
doing as well as could be expected
do justice to a dinner
Don't count your chickens before
 they are hatched.
don't rock the boat
doomed to disappointment
doom is sealed
doting parents
down and out
down life's pathway
down on my luck
down the drain
drastic shakeup
draw the line at
drop in the bucket
drop like flies
drug on the market
dry as a bone
dry as dust
due to the fact that
dull as dishwater
dull thud
dumb as an ox
dyed-in-the-wool

each and every
eager beaver
early bird catches the worm
easier said than done
easy as rolling off a log; easy as
 falling off a log
easy come, easy go
eat crow
eats like a horse
eats like a wolf
elevate an eyebrow
emerge unscathed

enchanted isle
enclosed herewith
enter the field of battle
equal to the occasion
errand of mercy
esteem it a great honor
eternal triangle
eternal verities
eternal vigilance
everything went along nicely
exception proves the rule
explore every avenue
extant
eyes bigger than his stomach
eyes like stars; starry-eyed;
 starry eyes; stars in her eyes

face the fact
face the music
facts of life
fair sex
faithful as a dog
faithful canine friend
fall down on the job
fall into the arms of Morpheus
fall like a ton of bricks
Familiarity breeds contempt.
far be it from me
far-reaching effects
fast and furious
fat as a pig
fat as butter
Father Time
favored us
feather in his cap
feather one's nest
fed up
feeling blue
feel in one's bones
feel like a million
feet of clay
fell madly in love
festive company
festive occasion

fettered soul
few and far between
fill the bill
filthy lucre
find favor
fine as silk
finer things of life
first and foremost
first flush of victory
fish out of water
fit as a fiddle
fit for a king
flat as a pancake
flat broke
flatly denied
floating on air
flowing with milk and honey
flying colors
flying high
fly in the ointment
fly into a rage
fly into the face of disaster
fly into the teeth of a storm
fly like a bird
fly off the handle
fond farewell
fond parents
food for thought
fools rush in
foregone conclusion
forlorn hope
for love or money
fortune smiled (or frowned)
free and easy
free as a bird
free as the breeze
free peoples of the world
fresh as a daisy
from A to Z
from that day forth
from time immemorial
from time to time
full flush of victory
furrowed brow

gala event; gala occasion; gala affair
gay Lotharios
generous to a fault
gentle as a lamb
get down to brass tacks
get down to business
get in there and fight
get the upper hand
ghost of a chance
gird my loins
Give it to us straight.
Give me your undivided attention.
give my right eye
give their all
give pause
glorious view
go down to posterity
go fly a kite
go my way
gone with the wind
good as gold
goodly number
Good Samaritan
good time was had by all
graceful as a swan
grand job
greased lightning
greatest of ease
great open spaces
greedy as pigs
green as grass
green thumb
green with envy
grievous error
Grim Reaper
grin and bear it
groaning board
grow by leaps and bounds
gutted by fire

hailed
hale and hearty

half the battle; won half the
  battle
happiest years of his life
happy as a lark
happy pair
hard as a rock
hard as nails
Haste makes waste.
haunts of men
have on good authority
head in the sand like an ostrich
heartfelt thanks
heart of gold
heart of the matter
heart's desire
heated argument
heavy as lead
he-man
herculean efforts
Hide your light under a bushel.
high and dry
high as a kite
His bark is worse than his bite.
his name is legion
history tells us
hit against a brick wall
hit an all-time low
hit below the belt
hit the ceiling
hit the hay
holding one's own
home beautiful
home sweet home
honest as the day is long
honest toil
Honesty is the best policy.
hops around like a sparrow
hot as hell
hotbed of intrigue
hourglass figure
hungry as a bear
hungry as wolves

I always say

I beg to remain
icy chill
icy stare
idle rich
I don't know whether I'm coming or going.
If a man is old enough to fight,
  he is old enough to vote.
if the truth be known
if worse comes to worst
Ignorance is bliss.
I haven't a minute to call my
  own.
imposing structure; imposing
  edifices
improve each shining hour
in all its glory
in a nutshell
in black and white
in conclusion
in connection with
industrious as an ant
inject a serious note
inner man
innocent as a newborn babe
in no uncertain terms
in one ear and out the other
in one fell swoop
in our time of need
in that case
in the last analysis; in the final
  analysis
in the nick of time
in the same boat
In the spring a young man's
  fancy turns to . . .
in this day and age
intestinal fortitude
intrepid fortitude
in view of the fact that
invite to partake
iron curtain of censorship
iron heel
iron out

irony of fate
I shudder to think what might have happened.
It all comes out in the wash.
it goes without saying
it's Greek to me
it is interesting to note
It never rains but it pours.
It's a small world.
It's not the heat; it's the humidity.
it stands to reason
ivory tower

jewel of a person

keep a civil tongue in your head
keep a stiff upper lip
keep a weather eye on
keep it under your hat
keep the wolf from the door
keep things humming
keep up with the Joneses
kickoff
kill the fatted calf
kill the motor
kill time
kind favor
knit my brows
knock on wood
knuckle down

labor of love
land-office business
last but not least
last mile
last rose of summer
last straw
lay it on with a trowel
lay the foundations
leaks like a sieve
lean and hungry look
lean as a pole
learn the ropes
leave no stone unturned

leaves much to be desired
led like sheep
lesser of two evils
let bygones be bygones
let's face it
let the cat out of the bag
let the matter drop
level best
level criticism
life of the party
light as a feather
limp as a dishrag
lion's share
literally
little by little
little hard cash
lock the barn door after the horse has been stolen
long arm of the law
long-felt want
look for support
look high and low
look like love's young dream
look like something the cat dragged in
loomed on the horizon
lose face
lose the thread of
Love is blind.
loved not wisely but too well
luxuriously appointed

mad as a hornet
mad as a wet hen
mad dash
majestic Mount _____
make a concerted effort
make a mountain out of a molehill
make contact with
make head or tail of
makes the world a better place to live in
malice aforethought
man in the street

manners of a pig
man's best friend
man-size job
mantle of snow
map out a plan
mark time
meek as a lamb
meets the eye
meet your Maker
memory of an elephant
mercury would soar into the 90's
meteoric career
method in his madness
mile a minute
milestone on the road of life
mince words
mind like a sponge
mind your P's and Q's
mine of information
miscarriage of justice
momentous decision
Money is the root of all evil.
more in sorrow than in anger
more sinned against than sinning
more than meets the eye
more the merrier
most unkind cut
Mother Nature; Mother Earth
multiply like rabbits
music hath charms
My love is like a red, red rose.
my one and only

nature's glory
naught but
neat as a pin
neck like a swan
needle in a haystack
needless to say
needs no introduction
nervous as a cat
nestled high in the mountains;
    nestling in the hills
never in the history of
never say die

new line of attack
news blackout
news leaked out
news spread like wildfire
night will fall
nipped in the bud
no action has been taken
nod approval
"No!" he snapped.
none the worse for wear
nose to the grindstone
no sooner said than done
Not a sound broke the stillness.
noteworthy achievement
no time like the present
now and then
now or never
nth degree
nutty as a fruitcake

ocean's roar
off the beaten track
oil-rich nation
old as Methuselah
old as the hills
old college try
old enough to be her father
old song and dance
ominous silence
on behalf of
once and for all
once upon a time
on the fence
on top of all this
out of a clear sky
out of the blue
over and above

pain in the neck
pall of smoke
partake of refreshments
part and parcel
parting of the ways
party was a washout
pass the time of day

patter of rain
pay the supreme penalty
peaches and cream
peal of thunder
pearls before swine
pearly gates
pearly teeth
people with whom he comes in
   contact
permit me to suggest
picture of despair
pins and needles
plain as day
playful as a kitten
playing second fiddle
play into the hands of
play possum
pleasant time was had by all
pleasing picture
pleasure and a privilege
plot thickens
pocket my pride
poignant stories
point the finger of suspicion
point with pride
Politics makes strange bedfel-
   lows.
poor as a church mouse
poor but honest
poor but proud
powers that be
pretty as a picture
pride and joy
Pride goeth before a fall.
production target
proud as a peacock
proud possessor; proud owner
psychological moment
pugilistic encounter
pull up stakes
pull your leg
pure and simple
pure as the driven snow
purse my lips
put in an appearance

put your shoulder to the wheel
put the horse before the cart
put your foot in your mouth

quaked in her boots
quick as a cat
quick as a flash
quick as a wink
quick like a bunny
quiet as a mouse
quiet enough to hear a pin drop

rack and ruin
raining cats and dogs
raining pitchforks
raison d'être
rakish angle
rank and file
rank outsiders
ran like a deer
rapt expression
raving beauties
razor's edge
reached its peak
read between the lines
rear its ugly head
recorded in blazing headlines
red as a beet
red as a rose
red-letter day
refresh my memory
reigns supreme
render inoperative
report progress
rest assured
retire to the sidelines
rich and varied experience
ride roughshod over
riot of color
riot-torn
ripe old age
risk life and limb
road to success is paved with
roll up a score
rotten to the core

royal reception
ruby lips
rude awakening
run amuck
run like a deer
running around like a chicken with its head cut off
runt of the litter

sadder but wiser
sad to relate
safe and sound
safe as a church
sail under false colors
salt of the earth
sands of time
save face
saving grace
saw the light of day
say the word
scarce as hen's teeth
scared out of his wits
scared to death
sea of faces
see eye to eye
Seeing is believing.
seek his fortune
sell like hotcakes
set the world on fire
settle his hash
seventh heaven
shadows of the goal post
shake a leg
sharp as a razor
sharp as a tack
shed light on the subject
She's a dreamboat.
shift into high gear
ship of state
shipshape and Bristol fashion
shoe the wild mare
shoot a glance
shot heard around the world
shot in the arm

sick as a dog
sigh of relief
sight unseen
silence being broken
silence reigned; silence reigned supreme
silhouetted against the sky
silly as a goose
sing like a bird
sinking fast
sink or swim
six of one, half-dozen of another
skeleton in the closet
skin like velvet
skinny as a rail
skin of his teeth
sky-high
skyrocketing costs
sleep like a dog
sleep like a log
sleep of the just
slick as a whistle
slippery as an eel
slow as cold molasses running uphill in January
slow but sure; slowly but surely
sly as a fox
smooth as glass
smooth as silk
snake in the grass
sneaking suspicion
snow job
snug as a bug in a rug
sober as a judge
social butterfly
social function
social whirl
socio-economic considerations
so far, so good
soft as silk
something tells me
so richly deserved
soup to nuts
sour grapes
speak in terms of

specimen of humanity
speculation is rife
spice of life
spreading a dragnet
spring chicken
square peg in a round hole
stab in the back
staff of life
stand my ground
stand shoulder to shoulder
stand us in good stead
status quo
steel himself
step in the right direction
stew in your own juice
stick to your guns
stiff as a poker
still as a mouse
Stitch in time saves nine.
stony silence
stood like a sentinel; stood like
    sentinels
straight and narrow
straight as an arrow
strange as it seems
strike while the iron is hot
strong as a lion
strong as an ox
stubborn as a mule
stuck-up
sturdy as an oak
sum and substance
sumptuous repast
supreme sacrifice
swan song
sweat of his brow
sweeping statement
sweet as honey
sweet as sugar
sweet fragrance of cherry blos-
    soms
sweet sixteen
sweet tooth
swim like a duck
swim like a fish

table groaned with food
tailor-made
take a dim view
take a firm grip
take into account
take into custody
take measure of
take my pen in hand
take my word for it
takes the cake
take stock
take the bitter with the sweet
take the bull by the horns
take things as we find them
take this opportunity
take to task
take with a grain of salt
tall, dark, and handsome
teeming millions
tendered his resignation
tender mercies
that's life
the fact that
the good life
the quick and the dead
The spirit is willing, but the
    flesh is weak.
the truth, the whole truth, and
    nothing but the truth
thin as a lath
thin as a rail
think things out
This is not always the case.
threadbare excuse
thread his way
threw me a curve
thrilled to
through thick and thin
throw caution to the wind
throw light on
throw the baby out with the
    bath water
thus I have shown
tide of battle
tight-lipped silence

tilting at windmills
Time and tide wait for no man.
time and time again
Time flies.
Time is money.
Time is ripe.
Time marches on.
time of my life
time-tested
tired as a dog; dog tired
tired but happy
to all intents and purposes
to each his own
To err is human, to forgive,
   divine.
toe the line
to go overboard
token of our appreciation
to make a long story short
to no avail
too funny for words
too good to be true
took his departure
to put it mildly
to some extent
to top it off
touch and go
tower of strength
treacherous as a snake
trial by fire
trials and tribulations
tried and true
trip the light fantastic
trite but true
troubled times
troubled waters
true-blue
Truer words were never spoken.
Truth is stranger than fiction.
turn over a new leaf
turn the tables
two peas in a pod

unable to see the woods for the
   trees

unaccustomed   (or   unworthy)
   as I am
undercurrent of excitement
under the weather
unleash the dogs of war
untimely death
untold agony
untold wealth
up in arms
upon the busy stage of life
upset the applecart
up to no good
use my head

vale of tears
Variety is the spice of life.
vast multitude
venture a suggestion
venture to predict
vicious circle
view with alarm
violence flowed
vise-like grip
voice like thunder

walk of life
warm as toast
water under the bridge
watery grave
wave of optimism
weaker sex
wealth of meaning
wear and tear
weather the storm
wee small hours
wended our way
wet behind the ears
what it boils down to
wheel of fortune
When the cat's away, the mice
   will play.
Where there's a will, there's a
   way.
whirlwind courtship
white as a sheet

white as snow
wide-open spaces
wild as an Indian
wind whispers through the trees
wise as an owl
with bated breath
without batting an eyelash
without rhyme or reason
withstand the test of time
wolfs down his food
word of mouth
words cannot express; words fail
to express; words failed;
words cannot describe; words
are inadequate
word to the wise

worked long and hard
worked to death
work like a beaver
work like a dog
work like a Trojan; work like
Trojans
works like a horse
world of the theatre
worse for wear
wreathed in smiles
wry jest

You can't take it with you.
You can't teach an old dog new
tricks.
You must not fail to come.

A
B
C
D
E
F
G
H
I
J